GW00673119

CHEESEWRING & SOUTH EAST CORNWALL

DEDICATED TO
Me Mum
Daisy E. F. Hawken

"CHEESEWRING & SOUTH EAST CORNWALL"

A Climbers' Guide

© Sean Hawken & Toni Carver

All rights reserved by individual contributors of photographs and on individual text contributions by writers other than the author.

First Edition published August 1998

Edited by Toni Carver

Designed and Typeset by Toni Carver

Printed and Published by:
The St. Ives Printing and Publishing Company,
High Street, St. Ives, Cornwall, TR26 1RS. UK.

ISBN 0 948385 26 X

Cover Photograph: Caroline Carpenter on Lemon Tree, *Hard Severe 4b* a '60's classic at Cheesewring Quarry. Photograph: Sean Hawken

Frontispiece: Malcolm Rescorle (leading) and Sean Hawken on Just Good Friends, *Very Severe 5a* at Trewortha Tor. Photograph: Andy Grieve

Back Cover: Nick Hancock on Northside Route 5c, The Cheesewring. Photograph: Andy Grieve

CHEESEWRING
& SOUTH EAST CORNWALL
A CLIMBERS' GUIDE
BY
SEAN HAWKEN

Editor: Toni Carver

Original Maps and Diagrams by Sean Hawken

With Photographs by
Andy Grieve, Nick Hancock, Sean Hawken and Peter Stanier

Additional graphic renderings and photo-repro by
Tobi Carver

The St. Ives
Printing and Publishing Company
High Street, St. Ives Cornwall, UK.

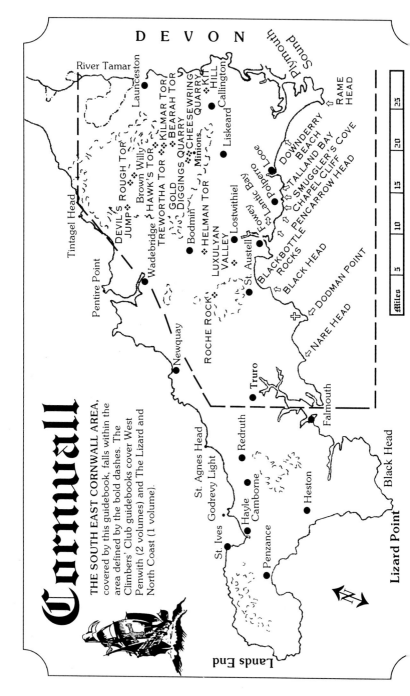

ACKNOWLEDGEMENTS

The author and editor gratefully acknowledge the generous help and assistance of all those who have contributed to, and consulted with us during the production of this guide. Our particular thanks to The Rt. Hon. The Lord Hunt, KG, CBE, DSO., Geoffrey Rees-Jones, Mrs. Charmion Fowler, Dr. Robert Romanis, Dr. Peter Stanier and Terry Goodfellow for their invaluable information and close collaboration in preparing the histories. To Pat Littlejohn and John Redhead whose views and comments helped form the editorial approach to the grading system. To Malcolm Rescorle, Mike Collier of Falmouth Coastguard and Capt. Phil Moran, Hon. Sec. St. Ives RNLI for casting a professional eye over the first aid and rescue notes and providing additional suggestions.

Our thanks to Andy Grieve for providing us with the benefit of his advice and his extensive knowledge on the climbing areas of South East Cornwall and for his constant and influential support. To Ken Palmer, Nick Hancock and Lee Earnshaw for their comments and advice and to all those who helped in checking route descriptions particularly: Caroline Carpenter, Malcolm Rescorle and Barnaby Carver.

To Trish and Barnaby Carver for sterling work proof reading through numerous revisions and to John Hunt and Robert Romanis, men both familiar with the business of publishing, who also undertook this work on the history section without even being asked! The chapter is immeasurably better for their contributions. We were particularly grateful for Lord Hunt's suggestion that we quote directly from his autobiography *Life is Meeting* where it was appropriate and for allowing us to do so.

Many thanks to Andy Grieve and Nick Hancock for their splendid photographs throughout the guide and to Geoffrey Rees-Jones and Peter Stanier for their photographs in the histories. Thanks to Bob Lambourne for his comments, information and for defining 'the criteria' for a British climbers' guidebook and to all those who sent in their route descriptions.

A special acknowledgement to Sean's mother, for supplying the flapjack to feed the deluge of climbers passing through the Hawken house. Also, for undertaking the enormous task of fuelling Andy Grieve's insatiable appetite, simply to keep him climbing new routes.

As well as the main contributors and helpers close to us there have been a veritable army of climbers and well-wishers who have thrown in helpful suggestions and advice on this project. To all those unnamed our thanks.

Like all modern guidebooks this one relies heavily on work that has gone before both for reference and clarification. Some previous publications and writers covering aspects of the climbing in South East Cornwall are:

Capt. D. G. Romanis's climbing diary known as;
The Red Book (private 1920s).

Climbers Club Journal 1923.

Oxford Mountaineering 1935.

London Mountaineering 1941.

Cornwall, A. W. Andrews & E. C. Pyatt (Climbers' Club 1950).

The Climbers Club Journals, 1965 & 1966.

Cornwall Vol 1, P. H. Biven & M. B. McDermott (Climbers' Club 1968).

A Climber in The West County, E. C. Pyatt (David & Charles 1968).

New Climbs 1970 editor: Ian Roper (Climbers' Club 1970).

The Minions Group in Cornwall, P. H. Stanier (private 1970).

Climbing in Cornwall, Carver, Stanier & Littlejohn (James Pike Ltd. 1973).

Climbing in Cornwall, New Climbs, Toni Carver (Minions Group 1974).

South-West Climbs, Pat Littlejohn (Diadem 1979)

The Work of Giants, Peter Stanier
(St. Ives Printing & Publishing Company 1988).

North Devon and Cornwall, Iain Peters (Climbers' Club 1988).

Climbing Guide to Dartmoor and the Cheesewring Quarry,
(3 Editions) by Paul Twomey, Tim Dennell and Lee Earnshaw
(Wide Blue Yonder 1990s).

The Minions Moor (second edition), Peter Stanier
(St. Ives Printing & Publishing Company. 1996).

CONTENTS

List of Illustrations

Nick Hancock on Mauritius (E5 6b/c) Cheesewring Quarry.   Photo: Andy Grieve

Andy Grieve coasteering at Pencarrow Head.   *Photo: Tom Galvin*

EDITOR'S NOTES,
CHANGING CLIMBS IN CHANGING TIMES

A FORTUITOUS meeting between the new guard and the ancient guard of Cheesewring men led to my editing this guidebook, some twenty two years after producing the first to the area. Sean Hawken had probably thought me dead! For this old fart to wander onto his sacred ground and casually solo 'a few old favourites' which, these days are far more often top roped than led must have seemed heresy! My last new route at Cheesewring had been in 1972, after which I gracefully faded away into the distant mists of the far West and the attractions of sea-kayaking and coasteering.

By virtue of an early start, I began climbing in 1959, I have been active through the greatest changes ever to have taken place in rock climbing. The most senior figures to have rolled up their sleeves and jumped in to help us with this guide have been John Hunt and Geoffrey Rees-Jones; the youngest have been keen teenagers. Between these generations there is a biblical life span which has allowed us a unique opportunity to take a broad historical overview and to cover the climbing history in great depth. The achievements of today are always based on those of folk who contributed in the past and it has been our view that they should not be forgotten in East Cornwall. Cheesewring, for example, has become a popular venue for present day serving marine commandos, often distanced from or unaware of the important role their predecessors played in the evolution of our sport. With accurate route descriptions and aided by a comprehensive history, our desire has been to achieve the standard of The Lambourne Criteria which states. "The defining feature of a British guidebook is that it should be a good read on the loo!" So we hope this will not just be a book for the crags!

ATTITUDES AND PERSPECTIVES

These have changed over time. With such changes climbing becomes increasingly vulnerable to misunderstandings, rancour and dispute. Such has been the case in West Penwith where, for over a decade, a bitter debate raged over different approaches to climbing. Traditional climbers versus sport climbing tactics and bolts! In past times climbers have viewed the best way of dealing with such matters as being a friendly debate in the pub, much the best way in my view. Please remember that the style of ascent is determined by the manner of the first led ascent. Unless you can repeat a climb in its original style, or improve on it, please respect the achievement of the first ascentionists. Enjoy it or leave it alone, don't mess about with it. If you do you will be spoiling the enjoyment of other climbers who don't necessarily share your views.

The Problem of the Present

Currently a number of issues are being debated in rock climbing and the first draft of these notes made a vain attempt to address them in some depth. This exercise was largely abandoned not out of any wide disagreement in the large body of opinion sampled, but more out of an understanding that some matters are not yet ready to be formalised in a guidebook. The scraping of British grades in favour of French grades on sport climbs is one good example and the use of the term *Headpointing* is another. Of particular concern is the way the grading system can become distorted when new, hard, traditionally geared climbs are extensively pre-practised before the first ground-up ascent. This has not yet become a problem in South East Cornwall where the division between the new and old climbing styles has been relatively clean cut. Hopefully this will remain the case with traditional climbs continuing to be produced without first ascentionists resorting to undeclared 'sport tactics.'

CLIMBING STYLES

Two distinct styles of climbing now exist in South East Cornwall, as elsewhere in Britain. Alongside *Traditional Style* climbs there are now the new *Sport Climbs*. The two styles have different ethics and considerations. The differences should be recognised and respected by all climbers.

Sport Climbs

The rationale behind sport climbing is that the highest standards can only be obtained by the comprehensive practising of specific sequences of hard moves. It is the unrestricted practising of moves before making an ascent of a climb that defines sport climbing (not the presence of bolts or insitu protection). Not being a sport climber myself the thing that impresses me most about the style is its inherent honesty. Sport climbs are evolved from projects. The line of the route is abseiled, cleaned and the protection (usually bolts) pre-placed to allow falls to be taken with minimal risk of injury. This style allows the climbers involved to practise the climb before the *redpoint* ascent which can sometimes take several days to achieve. The *redpoint* ascent is a bottom to top ascent without the leader taking a fall, resting on the rope or quick draws. The date of the first ascent is thus taken from the date of *redpoint* ascent, not the day of the first attempt. It is vitally important that the fixed protection on sport climbs and projects is not removed or interfered with since safety is paramount in this style which excels in achieving physical excellence in climbing.

Traditional Climbs.

Considerable trouble has been taken to bring the grades of the area's traditional climbs in line with climbs in other areas and current thinking on grading. The high ethical standards preferred by the local activists also usually ensures that the grade will be correct for a *ground-up, on-sight* ascent by visiting climbers familiar with the grade, even on relatively new climbs.

FIRST ASCENTS.

Most are, some are not! If you enter the new routing game make sure you write up a true and accurate record of your ascent with a concise description of your climb at the time. Get your partner/s to check the description and, if possible friends to agree its accuracy, climb your route and confirm its grade. Lodge copies with the climbing magazine of your choice, your climbing club and the people most likely to produce the next guide to the area. When doing this work leave your ego at home! Adopt this *modus operandi* and all guidebook writers and editors will be eternally grateful.

Retro-claiming climbs is generally a serious mistake. Memory is a very fickle thing so the practice breeds distrust. If you are a well known new router your action will be seen as 'out of character' and arouse suspicion - all the more so if you are known to usually keep good records. I can think of several climbs I was too lazy to write-up that were later climbed by others, well done to those who care enough to do the job properly. Conversely, If you develop an area and find climbers that remember doing climbs there previously, but are reliant solely on their memory, write up your ascent as a recorded ascent giving as much ascent history as you can piece together. As climbing becomes ever more popular this type of 'good practice' will become increasingly valuable.

PITONS AND BOLTS.

Both pitons and bolts, when used as insitu protection, should not be stolen or damaged. Such theft and vandalism compromises safety and may be considered as an 'act of reckless endangerment'. However, deteriorating pitons should be removed once there is no longer any chance of damaging the rock. Basically, pitons are bad news and it is always preferable to find standard gear placements. If left permanently in place the security they afford becomes extremely dubious while if hammered in and out of rock they will split, damage and break it. Many old artificial climbs now go free simply because the brutal practices of the old 'whack and dangle' boys created holds and nut placements for the free climbers who came later.

Bolts are generally better news; when used at agreed sport venues. The standard bolts are glued in, not easily disguised and are only resorted to when no other form of protection is available. At the time of writing there is a general acceptance in Cornwall that only quarries provide suitable venues for the bolt, especially in South East Cornwall! Unlike a piton, a bolt will be safer insitu and last longer if competently placed. More importantly, less damage will be done to the rock. On natural crags traditional climbers object to damage caused by pegs and bolts largely on visual and environmental grounds. Quarry climbers, however, lose quality climbing when the rock, which erodes quite quickly anyway, is carelessly damaged. When a bolt is properly maintained or even properly removed the remaining hole can be filled with either a compound of resin and local powdered rock or Plasticine which will attract lichen.

On no account should you place a bolt or piton on an existing route which other climbers have always managed to do without. Back off and find a climb of a standard you can manage or top rope it until you feel you can do it without need of a hammer and drill. Bolts are, on rare occasions, placed retrospectively on quarry climbs when a consensus of local climbers feel there is a good reason to do so.

Never 'chop' a bolt unless you are part of a consensus group who agree that adequate alternative protection has been found to render the bolt redundant. Also remember that insitu protection not only provides runners but also guidebook reference points and that confusion can also increase risk! Usually a bolt will have been placed only after careful consideration by the first ascentionist. The bolt might offend, but if you chop it you will really upset the climbers who want to do the route! A far worse potential evil is knowing that bolts have been wilfully 'chopped' climbers will attempt the climb with the rock shattering piton.

CHIPPING HOLDS

Oh, abominable practice, disavowed even by those who do it! There are two great do nots here. Don't manufacture a hold and don't accuse anyone else of doing so unless you have seen them and have witnesses! Where the limit of this rare but objectionable practice lies can only rest with the individual climber. Where does vigorous 'cleaning' end and chipping begin? Difficult decisions that must rest with the originator of a route. Develop a conscience!

CHANGING GRADES

Changing attitudes, over time, have impacted seriously on the traditional grading system. Many of today's *E2* leaders would be hard pressed to get up a 1920's *Very Severe* if they had to climb it using the equipment of that period. Who even remembers how to climb in nails these days? The vast improvements in protection methods and equipment mean, simply, that it is much easier to do the same climb in the 90s than it was in the 60s. I would personally estimate the gain in common standards afforded by the technical improvements to be about three full grades and the safety gain much higher. Perversely the tendency has always been to upgrade troublesome old climbs rather than downgrade them as climbing has become safer and easier. I see this as a very worrying trend. It creates doubt and illusion and seems to be driven by the demands of commercialism rather than by the need of the majority climbers for a stable and trusted system. It is well beyond the scope of this guide to get involved in this debate. Sean has, however, introduced some 'optional extras' to the grading system which I am sure will assist you in selecting suitable climbs. He has also made a tremendous effort to standardise grades throughout this guide in line with other areas. Enjoy!

Toni Carver - *April 1998*

BRITISH GRADES & THEIR INTERNATIONAL EQUIVALENTS

German	Great Britian Traditional	GB Tech	French	USA	Aussie	Swedish	Czech
III	Easy & Moderate (1 - 2a)	1	1	5.0	2	3-	
III+	Difficult (2b - 2c)	2a		5.1	3 / 4	3	
IV-	Hard Difficult (3a)	2b	2	5.2	5 / 6	3+	
IV	Very Difficult (3b - 3c)	2c		5.3	7	4-	
	Hard Very Difficult (3c - 4a)	3a			8		
IV+	Mild Severe (4a)	3b	3	5.4	9 / 10	4	
V-	Severe (4a - 4b)	3c		5.5	11	4+	
V	Hard Severe (4b)	4a		5.6	12 / 13	5-	
	Mild Very Severe (4b - 4c)	4b	4c	5.7	14	5	
V+	Very Severe (4b - 5a)		4c+ / 5a / 5a+		15		
VI-	Hard Very Severe (4c - 5b)	4c	5b / 5b+	5.8	16 / 17	5+	VI / VII
VI	Extremely Severe, E1 (4c - 5c)	5a	5c / 5c+ / 6a	5.9	18	6-	VIIa / VIIb
VI+					19		VIIc
VII-	E2 (5b - 5c)	5b	6a+ / 6b	5.10a / 5.10b	20	6	VIII
VII			6b+	5.10c		6+	VIIIa
VII+	E3 (5c - 6a)	5c	6c / 6c+	5.10d / 5.11a	21 / 22	7-	VIIIb
VIII-				5.11b	23	7	VIIIc
VIII	E4 (5c - 6b)	6a	7a / 7a+	5.11c / 5.11d	24	7+	
VIII+	E5 (6a - 6c)	6b	7b / 7b+ / 7c	5.12a / 5.12b / 5.12c / 5.12d	25 / 26 / 27	8- / 8	
IX-							
IX	E6 (6a - 6c)	6c	7c+ / 8a / 8a+	5.13a / 5.13b / 5.13c	28 / 29	8+ / 9-	
IX+							
X-	E7 (6b - 7a)	7a	8b / 8b+	5.13d / 5.14a / 5.14b	30 / 31 / 32	9	
X							
X+	E8/E9 (7a - 7b+)	7b	8c / 8c+	5.14c / 5.14d	33	9+	

The traditional British adjectival grades are shown with the technical (numerical) grades they are most usually associated with (see *The Grading System* in the Introduction).

INTRODUCTION

SOUTH EAST CORNWALL has a rich variety of developed climbing. Geologically there is a diversity of rock quality ranging from the reliable solid granite of the Cheesewring Quarry and weathered, heavily crystalline granite, (Dartmoor type) of the wind swept Bodmin Moor Tors to the vast mix of schists, shales and slates of the South Coast. The granites require little or no cleaning even on routes or boulder problems which have never, or only rarely, been climbed and loose holds are rare. If you have a yearning for something out of the ordinary, try the wonderful and weirdly formed holds that abound on the tourmaline of Roche Rock, also a sound and reliable rock, but always beware of the unexpected even on well trodden trade routes.

In contrast, The South Coast has an awesome reputation for loose rock. This is more than justified for many cliffs but to dismiss the special adventure of climbing here would do a disservice to some of the area's earliest pioneers! Several cliffs, that may have a sprinkling of loose rock, scream epic saga! So, to those men and women who still retain a modicum of adventurous spirit in their climbing, I take my hat off to you.

One place that was nearly kept out of the guide, to ensure no crowds, was the superb location of Downderry Beach. The bouldering here is excellent and plentiful and as long as you stay on the selected problems, you will find the rock firm and acceptable. For those who tire easily of the same scenery there are many points of interest to explore, not mentioned in this guide. Remember to check the rock quality first, or you could be in for a surprise.

DESCRIPTIONS

The climbing areas are divided into three main groupings; the granite quarries, the Bodmin Moor Tors and the South Coast, each region's venues are presented, more or less, from east to west as you enter Cornwall thereby considering the visitor. Generally climbs are described around the cliffs from left to right unless it is more natural to describe them right to left as at Roche Rock in which case the change is stated.

THE GRADING SYSTEM

In an attempt at achieving consistency some climbers will no doubt notice changes from previous guides. These alterations have been made after further ascents of climbs with controversial grades and advice has been taken from as many of the area's climbers as possible. The amended grading is intended, and believed, to bring the grades in alignment with the rest of the area and hopefully most of the country. An innovation, that of a protection grade, has been included to assist you in your choice of route. It has been kept simple so as not to take the adventure out of the climbs while, hopefully, addressing the problems of grade interpretation in an area with so many different sorts of climbing.

The new Protection Grades

Important note: The following grading system presumes the leader is competent at placing protection and leading the grade chosen.

(NP) no protection.

(PP) poorly protected.

(AP) adequate protection.

(WP) well protected.

Traditional grades

The traditional grading system, encompassing the realignments, has been used here conventionally, as it would be in other British guidebooks. The assumption here is for an on-sight lead by a climber competent at the grade. A *Very Severe* leader, for example, should be able to feel confident that he has a good chance of climbing any *VS* in the guide from the ground up. If a visiting leader is really only happy on well protected *Very Severe* the new protection grade will save time when choosing an appropriate climb.

The E grades

For young or new climbers, it is important to gain a full comprehension of the British grading system at the "extreme" end of the grading scale, before embarking upon any on-sight climbing.
Today's E-grades have evolved by 'custom and usage' out of the

original single old grade of Extreme into a whole subsystem. The E-grade system now works thus: The higher the E-grade the more arduous the climbing i.e. *E2 5c* would suggest challenging climbing, but for those generally capable of 5c it would imply relative safety. When an adjoining technical grade is low, relative to a higher E-grade i.e. *E4 5c* this proposes that the overall climbing is likely to be very arduous and an error of judgement could have serious consequences. These climbs should be left to the experienced or at least be very carefully considered.

Exceptionally Severe

If you happen upon one of the few routes graded "*Exceptionally Severe*" (*XS*) this denotes a particularly lethal cocktail of extreme climbing on loose rock (only for the terminally insane). On an *XS* a hold snapping or a leader fall might result in fatal consequences for the entire party!

Sport Grades

Where a sport climb, that is to say a climb that has been worked out as a project until a *redpoint* (ground up, no falls, clipping the quickies to the bolts as you go) ascent, is described the French grading system has been used ahead of the British system which is shown in brackets. Where the British grade is shown ahead of a bracketed French grade this implies a bolt protected but (loosely) traditional style route — since placing bolts inevitably involves a lot of hanging around the degree of pre-working may not be known. As a rule of thumb, sport climbs would also tend to show the new *(WP)* grade. Anything less than *(WP)* might imply old bolts, bad insitu gear or even risk of injury from a bad fall stopped by a bolt runner. Being brought up horizontally in the small of the back after a fall from an overhang, for example.

Star Grades

At last! A system that works really well! Used here as everywhere else. Three stars awarded for the exceptional climbs, two for the best and one for the good.

Marrying up the Systems

The guide also contains a Universal Grading Chart for the use of the foreign globe-trotting climber, who no doubt has a terrible time with our traditional grading system. The chart was also essential for the coverage of the French graded sport climbs, where they occur in the guide. While there is a growing school of thought that feel sport climbs should only carry French grades we realised that the time has not yet come for this and it may not suit everyone to see these routes without the British grading or to be European! As stated above, you will see the supposed British equivalent for sport climbs in brackets next to the French grading.

LEAVE NO TRACE!

Try to avoid the need to defecate around the crags. This is a bad habit that seems to afflict climbers more than most and in such beauty spots toilet paper blowing in the wind is so ugly. If you can't help but go, find somewhere off the beaten track and carefully burn the toilet paper without starting a fire! If possible bury your by-product. Finally, always take your litter home.

DISCLAIMER

Climbing is a dangerous sport, climbing near the sea even more so. You do it entirely at your own risk and while every care has been taken to ensure that the content of the guidebook is accurate, please note the word 'guide'. Climbers' guidebooks let you know what has been climbed, where it is and what you are likely to encounter on your adventures. Such books are not instruction manuals and can never be a substitute for sound judgement and experience. We take no responsibility for your safety, you climb because you want to, at your own cognisance and at your own risk.

Access

At, and up until the time of writing, no real difficulties have been encountered over access in South East Cornwall. Experience has shown that if you cause no damage, behave well and leave no traces behind you, then you will not be unwelcome. However, both landowners and their attitudes change and are not always consistent. Climbers should check the current position over access for any given area at the time of their visit. If in doubt - check it out. A guidebook is not a passport!

HISTORY NOTES – ANCIENT

Toni Carver

Moorlanders

THANKS TO A wonderfully curious expedition South East Cornwall can legitimately claim the oldest recorded rock climb in Great Britain. However, the unsuspecting 'mountaineer' was in that great early tradition of adventurous men climbing in pursuit of a 'scientific' or some other goal. In the case of Thomas Bond climbing proved to be a necessary evil in his quest for 'druidical basins'.

Such basins abound atop the moorland tors of the Granite Kingdom and are natural features formed by wind swirling water and pebbles around in small depressions, eventually eroding out the perfect basin. They make great 'thank God!' holds. In the eighteenth century the prevailing theory was that the ancient Celtic priesthood had made the basins to collect baptismal water which they showered on their congregations assembled below the tors for blessing.

In 1802, Thomas Bond and his mounted party rode up onto East Bodmin Moor from the South. First their guide took them to see the abandoned dwelling of the first 'Cheesewring' man, Daniel Gumb. Gumb was then, as he is today, a legendary figure in East Cornwall. Born around 1700 in Linkinhorne parish he achieved early celebrity because of his remarkable love of reading and considerable knowledge of mathematics. Bred a stonecutter he liked to work the high moors where he had the quietude to think.

While working on the South side of Stowes Hill, now the void of Cheesewring Quarry, Gumb had come across a vast block which he excavated beneath to make a dwelling, lining the interior with stone cemented with lime. His idea was to create a secluded habitation suitable for study. While Gumb would, of necessity, have been an active 'boulderer' (that he achieved a technical grade of 7b by the year 1740 is a complete fabrication) his relevance to climbing history here rests on his long standing reputation as Cornwall's 'Mountain Philosopher' whose house became a chapel and observatory from which, 'He was never known to descend from the craggy mountain on which it stood to attend worship.'

When Bond viewed Gumb's dwelling it was still intact. *"When we reached Cheesewring our guide led us to the house of Daniel Gumb cut by him out of solid granite. This artificial cavern was about 12 feet deep and not quite so broad.....on the right-hand side of the door was carved "D. Gumb 1735."* Like all who encounter the story of the enigmatic Gumb, Bond enquired about his character: *"The guide told us Gumb was accounted a pretty sensible man. I have no hesitation in saying he must have been a pretty eccentric character to have dwelt for several years with his wife and children, several of whom were born and died here."* Sadly Gumb's house with its original 35ft., long roof slab was destroyed by quarrying in 1870. However, an example of his Euclidean mathematical jottings still survives in stone carvings that can be found on the roof of his restored 'house' near Cheesewring quarry.

On the 6th of August 1802, having ridden to Kilmar from Cheesewring, Thomas Bond made his mark in the history of Cornish Climbing. Hunting for that druidical basin he and his friend climbed the leaning tower at the western end of the tor naming it *The Western Turret* next they tackled *The Eastern Turret* which is where Bond discovered the thrill of climbing.

After a terrifying crawl under the overhangs — in fear of breaking their pocket watches – they considered the summit push. *"We examined the rocks above us, in order to observe the best mode of ascending them. I first made the ascent, and in the uppermost rock, discovered the largest Druidical basin we had met with, and observed it had a lip, or channel facing the South. The horrid precipices on either side prevented me from getting to the top of this rock, as I felt a slight vertigo. I then got down on a lower rock, and my friend ascended the uppermost one, and not finding himself dizzy, got into the basin itself (where I hope he will never go again), and waved his hat to our companions below."* After waving the hat Bond's friend measured the prized druidical basin with his riding whip before making the descent which marked Bond's swansong to his newly discovered activity: *"I believe nothing will ever induce me to pay a second visit to the top of this rock."*

Bond's belief in druidical basins presupposes that he assumed these tors had been climbed many times, certainly by druids! The Cornish, by virtue of their traditional professions: mining, fishing, smuggling, sheep farming etc., have always been ardent scramblers and even in today's climate of hard technical problems it is still a mistake to underestimate the abilities of former men. This is particularly true in an area where the reticent Victorians of the alpine golden age, came and went largely unmarked. Sir Leslie Stephen, for example had a second home in Cornwall and was familiar with the county for some forty years. And; of an area that waited 118 years before anyone else bothered to write up a climb!

Climbers and Gunners

Suddenly in the early 1920s there was an unprecedented burst of activity from Donald Romanis and Sir Bertrand Jerram. Nare Head was climbed and explored, *Chapel Chimney* on the sea cliffs near Polperro and the classic *South East Climb* at the Devil's Jump were ascended while Roche Rock was realised as a fine climbing venue. Romanis explored Carmears Rocks in the Luxulyan Valley recording an ascent of *The Waterfall Slabs* on the right of the rocks and noting the possibilities of the chimneys to the left. The pair were local to the area and Donald Romanis in particular ranged far and wide through South East Cornwall and up to Dartmoor with little regard for rock quality.

Bertrand Jerram's father was The Rector of Talland church, near Polperro, where the Romanis family rented a small holiday cottage on the south-west side of Talland beach which they visited every year. Donald's father, a housemaster at Charterhouse had to retire from teaching because of ill-health. He became the Preacher of the Charterhouse, in London. He had to go to great trouble to preserve his cottage, which he may have eventually bought. First it was necessary to build a sea wall to protect it from erosion but this was allowed to decay and the cottage and garden eventually slipped into the sea. Talland Bay, small enough today, was a tiny community in the 1890s and the boys became friends from early childhood.

Peter Biven in his 1968 Climbers' Club guide Cornwall Volume 1, which included Roche and Cheesewring, speculated that the pair might have been the first to climb in Cheesewring quarry: *"First in 1899, as boys, and later in 1921 making a more serious attempt at climbing."* It was an unlikely statement because in 1899 the boys were still two or three years off their 10th birthdays while in 1921 the cliff was a fully industrialised working quarry. Biven, however, would not have been far off the mark as the boys seem to have been natural climbers and soon got to know the moors and shores of their native South East Cornwall.

Both men had distinguished careers that took them far from home. Jerram was a diplomat in the Levantine Service and Romanis a professional soldier in the Royal Artillery, *the Gunners.* Both became caught up in the Russian Revolution of 1917. Jerram was taken prisoner by the Bolsheviks in Moscow, while by a curious twist of fate Donald Romanis also had to deal with the Bolsheviks. Taking part in the allied landings at Archangel, he was seconded to the White Russian armies in charge of a special rapid fire gun which he transported around Russia on a railway carriage. It was after these adventures that the friends found themselves together at home again - climbing.

Captain Romanis was briefly stationed at Falmouth when the Roche climbs were made: *"My friend Jerram and I had often visited the place, but its climbing possibilities only occurred to us after we had tasted the delights of the granite coast near the Land's End. Wicca Cove, I think it was, that made us think of Roche and before long we managed several afternoons there, Jerram coming from Polperro, twenty-five miles away on the South Coast, and myself motorcycling up from Falmouth, an equal distance in the opposite direction. As a result of our exploration we came to the conclusion that we had found the ideal place for a day's climbing picnic."*

The Romanis family are of Scots descent, south of the border now for five generations. Donald's brother William Hugh Cowie Romanis was also a climber and the brothers climbed together in the Alps before The Great War. Overseas for most of his soldiering life Romanis saw both India and China. He climbed whenever he could and wherever he was stationed including the Himalaya.

In Cornwall the climbs and explorations he recorded with Jerram seem to be the product of a unique period when the friends had some respite in their busy lives. By then the Romanis home was Donald's mother's house, built in the 1920s some years after the death of her husband, which superceded the original cottage. It was to here that Donald returned on leave and the family enjoyed their reunions. On these occasions he would take the youngsters in the family on to the moors where he was not always the most impressive of solo climbers. His daughter, Charmion, recalls that on two occasions he got himself stuck on Vixen Tor, Dartmoor and on another fell and broke his arm while bouldering on Kilmar!

Romanis left the army, around 1936 and went into the RAF as an intelligence officer but as soon as the Second World War started he rushed back to his guns. Too old for regimental duties he was employed as staff officer, continuing with intelligence and communications work. After the war he retired with the rank of Major but sadly he died in 1949 in his mid-fifties, an early age at which other South West climbers, notably Admiral Keith Lawder (of Lundy and Devon fame), were just starting their climbing careers. Sir Bertrand Jerram had better luck , living on until 1971.

In the 1930s, it was Roche that again attracted attention; this time from David Cox, the 'indefatigable' explorer of Dartmoor and the Dewerstone, hot on the trail of Romanis and Jerram. In Roche, Cox noted similarities with the Dewerstone but a comment from the time. *"For the most part the rocks are very steep, but every now and then the climber comes across odd knobs and pockets which give remarkably good holds,"* suggests the pockmarked crag has been growing pockets over the years! His contribution of 1933 was *Oxford Climb* and when war broke out Cox, like Romanis before him, became a Gunner.

Commandos: Climbing in the War Years

There is a great failing among those of us who write climbing histories to concentrate only on those who record first ascents which are often only the result of some greater process of history. During the war years the foundations of modern rock climbing were laid and the way post war climbers were to learn their skills became established. More people than ever before became climbers. Many soldiers and marines, particularly the instructors, grew to value and love the activity for its own sake. From their contribution the patterns of post war 'adventure training' evolved.

In this respect the role of Cornwall is unique in climbing history although the story closely links us with Scotland. If by virtue of the Georgian 'moorlanders' South East Cornwall can loosely claim the first recorded rock climbs, then it can also claim to be the home of this wartime revolution that changed the face of climbing in the 1940s, '50s and '60s

In 1940, following the fall of France and the German occupation of Europe, it occurred to a so far unidentified, 'someone' that we had no mountain warfare troops. Climbing troops would be useful for fighting through strongly held mountain terrain in occupied Europe or possibly to open up a second front in Norway. Who, and at what level of command these thoughts were processed remains a mystery but the realisation led to a 'note' being passed around the early Commando units, all of which were army, requesting anyone with a knowledge of climbing to make themselves known to the War Office.

The request came to the attention of Geoffrey Rees-Jones serving with No 5 Commando. While a teacher at Eastborne College Rees-Jones had been taught his climbing skills by the chemistry master there, a keen climber by the name of Snell. For his first climb Snell took Rees-Jones up *Intermediate Gully* on Dow Crag, above Coniston in the Lake District. Nailed boots, a stiff hemp rope, a steel karabiner and a piton or two were the only items of equipment used for rock climbing before the war, and pitons were frowned on then too!

Rees-Jones volunteered his skills and found himself stationed at the Clachaig Hotel in Glen Coe with three or four other Commando Officers who had responded to the note. Also in the group was Sandy Wedderburn, a former president of Cambridge Mountaineering Club, the most experienced climber among them. For three months these officers ran a course a month selecting and retaining the promising climbers to help make the next course bigger. At the end the officers sent their report to the War Office. The report concluded that it was possible to make a mountaineering soldier out of an ordinary squaddy.

When Rees-Jones returned to 5 Commando, the unit, which had been shifted around from Yorkshire to the South Coast had settled in Falmouth. For the second time in twenty years an army

Sir Bertrand Jerram leading the traverse on South East Buttress at Roche Rock (circa 1921).

Donald G. Romanis

State of the art climbing footwear, circ 1943. "Standard issue! No soldiers vibrams here," Rees-Jones wrote on the back of this photograph used to brie new arrivals.

Geoffrey Rees-Jones

"The splendid men out on an afternoc jolly!" Was how Rees-Jones captioned the photograph of his CMWTC commandc bouldering near St. Ives in 1943.

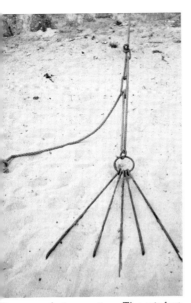

Commando innovation. The gripfast, a belay that even worked on sand!

Assault technique, or as Rees-Jones preferred to put it. "The less able climbers on fixed ropes."

Commando Sgt. Charlesworth demonstrating 'correct' climbing posture.

Legendary commando instructor, Joe Barry, confidence building whilst sending a signal to the Germans. Barry did not believe climbers should record climbs.

Supreme confidence lay at the bas of commando climbing theory. Goc leaders were expected to know the limitations and never fall. Stead nerves were all important and nor were steadier than Joe Barry's.

Early days at Cheesewring Quarry a place pronounced "pretty grim!" t Commando Instructor Jim Smith (left) during a visit in 1965 with Richa Grose (centre) and Toni Carver of the Truro School Rock Climbing Club.

captain stationed at Falmouth was to have a major impact on the future of Cornish climbing – although he never bothered recording one single route!

Having been climbing solidly for three months, Rees-Jones managed to persuade his commanding officer to let him train his troop for cliff assault when, seemingly out of the blue, one of the great mountaineering figures of the day, Professor Noel Odell, materialised. Odell is best remembered for his part in the ill-fated British Everest Expedition of 1924. When George Leigh-Mallory and Andrew Irvine disappeared near the summit, Odell who because of greater mountaineering experience and better acclimatization should have perhaps accompanied Mallory on the summit attempt, was the last man to see them alive. The expedition geologist, he had trailed behind the summit party to collect specimens. It was, in fact, geology that had first brought him to Cornwall when as a student he worked in the mines around Camborne in 1914. Noel Odell had also been a soldier in the First World War and had been wounded twice. By the time he was stationed at Falmouth he was 51, no longer a young man!

Rees-Jones never quite knew how he 'got tangled up with Noel' or why Odell came to be with 5 Commando but in a letter to Toni Carver (16/10/72) Odell explained. *"In 1941, when I was a Capt. R.E., and on the staff of Future Operations and Plans (F.O.P.S), I was attached for a time to No 5 Commando (Army), stationed at Falmouth. Our training programme for coastal assault exercises took us mainly to Bosigran or other Penwith Cliffs. But with one of the Commando's officers, Capt. Geoffrey Rees-Jones (incidentally an Oxford Rugger (sic) Blue and Welsh International) I made an extensive reconnaissance round most of the coast of Cornwall and part of Devon, to examine useful cliffs for training. We did some 'scrambles' but I am afraid recorded no specific routes."*

By the time of the reconnaissance Rees-Jones had already based himself at Bosigran Count House in West Penwith having met 'The Father of Cornish Climbing' Arthur Andrews. Andrews had shown him 'a few good places' for No 1 Troop to train. The Troop also gave a demonstration, "to a whole lot of bloody generals in the most stupid places," says Rees-Jones. It was about this time he linked up with Odell.

One experience vividly recalled by Rees-Jones on the 'recces' occurred not in South East Cornwall, but in South Devon. "We did a walk between Bolt Head and Bolt Tail. It was a bloody hot day, and we were walking along having a look down. We both had ropes and it was so hot that Noel said, 'It's much better to wear your shirt outside your trousers.' So we were walking along with our shirts outside our trousers carrying climbing ropes." The pair finished the recce of this section of coast and returned to Falmouth, but. "Considerably later on, in 1944, we were doing a 'show' at Salcombe and a policeman came up and said: "I wonder if you can help me," because we were wearing commando stuff and so on. He had a file about a mile deep about all this. I said: "Yes, that was me and Noel Odell!" They had thought we were German spies! Landed there by submarine or something".

At this point the war rudely interrupted any climbing developments that might have resulted from these coastal explorations. 5 Commando was sent to invade Madagascar. At 2.00am Rees-Jones took in his troop. His was the first landing craft in and he was the first man ashore, catching the Vichy French 'with their trousers down.' They successfully captured the battery overlooking the bay where the task force was to follow. Homeward bound again Rees-Jones and his troop were stopped at Cape Town, South Africa, not a man to miss an opportunity he continued climbing, training his commandos on Table Mountain.

With military climbing on the threshold of a new dawn as 5 Commando began assaulting the Penwith cliffs and Rees-Jones and Odell's fashion sense caused consternation among the Salcombe spy-catchers, South East Cornwall was not to miss out altogether. In 1941. R. G. Folkard, made his own reconnaissance of the East Bodmin Moor Tors visiting Kilmar, Trewortha, Bearah and Hawk's Tor where he recorded eleven climbs. Unlike Thomas Bond, Folkard was no hunter of druidical basins but enjoyed discovering them for himself. *"The top surfaces are frequently pitted with potholes, probably largely caused by wind erosion. They are remarkably regular in shape and usually circular. In size they vary from a few inches to over three feet in diameter. Their depth is eighteen inches."* It seems he was able to estimate this without the aid of a riding whip!

Rees-Jones returned to Britain at the end of 1942 to find that in his absence Headquarters Combined Operations had set up The Commando Mountain and Snow Warfare Training Centre at Braemar in the Cairngorms. The Commandant was the Himalayan mountaineer Frank Smythe. The Chief Instructor John Hunt, now Lord Hunt (leader of the successful 1953 British Everest Expedition). Geoffrey Rees-Jones joined the three other instructors: David Cox, Theo Nicholson and Alan Greenhalgh. The permanent staff was formed by men from Scottish Command and the centre's original purpose was to train commando troops to fight in high snow covered mountains.

On the face of it Frank Smythe seemed a most curious choice to have headed up the centre. A Squadron Leader, invalided out of the RAF in 1927 when his doctor cautioned him to walk up stairs slowly for the rest of his life; he went on to become one of the best known Himalayan climbers of the 1930s. Smythe organised the successful Kamet expedition in 1931 and had been on Everest with Eric Shipton in 1933 when he equalled Norton's 28,000ft., height record of 1924. He was on the Everest expedition of 1936 and, perhaps significantly, with Odell on the 1938 expedition. Frank Smythe also had a good record of Alpine ski tours and was a prolific mountaineering writer. How Smythe came to command the CMSWTC remains a mystery.

John Hunt, the first professional soldier to appear on the scene, recalls. "The whole outfit was pretty indifferently managed by dear Frank who was a delightful chap but he was no leader in that sense. It wasn't a particularly military outfit and I was supposed to put some reality into it." Smythe was, "not particularly interested in training the soldiers. He was very interested in taking them on walks he liked himself." Although younger than his friend Noel Odell, Frank Smythe was in his early forties at this time and, as Hunt comments in his book *Life is Meeting: "a gentle, most unwarlike character, whose main contribution to the work at the Centre was to impart his deep, poetic love of the mountains to the tough, high spirited wearers of the Green Beret."*

Unwarlike though he was, Smythe loathed what the Germans had done to his sport as *"Hitlerism spread into mountaineering."* In his book *British Mountaineers* which was published by William

Collins in 1942 he wrote. *"I first became cognisant of it during the International Kangchenjunga Expedition of 1930 when every member was issued with a flag which he was expected to keep flying over his tent. It was the ambition of the Germans to plant their flags on the top of each mountain. The emblem issued to me was a Union Jack with the stripes the wrong way round, made in Germany. Running short of pocket handkerchiefs on one occasion I used it as a substitute to the horror of my German companions. Possibly, indeed, the alleged decay of democracy dates from this."*

John Hunt, in his early thirties when he arrived at the Braemar centre, had utilised *"the privileged life of a British Army Officer in India between the wars"* to build up a formidable catalogue of mountaineering experience. In 1940, completely independently of the Commando initiative, he had been able to put into practise his own belief in the value of preparing troops for war by training them in mountain terrain. Major Hunt persuaded his brigade commander to let him run a 'toughening up course' for selected officers and men from the Helyg mountain hut in Snowdonia. For instructors he enlisted the help of fellow climbers, among them Wilf Noyce and Alf Bridge. Hunt judged his course a success and sent a report to Geoffrey Winthrope-Young, then president of the Alpine Club, who in turn forwarded it to Kurt Hahn the founder of Gordonstoun School. Later this contact was to have tremendous implications in post-war youth adventure training.

Hunt and his fellow instructors managed to put the missing 'realism' in the unit but after about six months of training Nos 1,4 and 12 Commando a decision was taken not to use commandos for mountain warfare and the unit seconded to train the Lovat Scouts as a mountaineering battalion. Frank Smythe left for Canada, to set up mountain training for the Lovat Scouts there. Hunt was recalled to his regiment in Egypt leaving Rees-Jones in command.

Training the Lovat Scouts took place in North Wales over the last four months of 1943, when the bulk of holds on Tryfan disappeared under the crunch of the Tricouni! Rees-Jones managed to 'fiddle' Sandy Wedderburn, the most experienced climber from the original course, as his second in command. Rees-Jones maintains he needed Wedderburn because. "He was sufficiently Scottish and the hierarchy of the Lovats was rather better at shooting grouse than climbing mountains!" The unit trained 700 men in elementary mountain craft, and a nucleus of rock climbers, before sending them on to the Canadian Rockies where they learnt snow-craft and skiing. Later in Greece The Lovat Scouts, complete with their skis, replaced the 2nd Cameron Highlanders in John Hunt's brigade. He continued with their training on Mount Olympus and later they fought very successfully in Italy.

John Hunt feels that a great opportunity was lost in these early years of mountain warfare training and that the War Office never realised the potential. In *Life is Meeting* he records that within six weeks of leaving Braemar he found himself fighting in Italy where specialised troops might have made a significant difference. The allies spent the winter of 1943/44 held back by the German forces defending the eighty five miles of the 'Gustav line' which stretched across the spine of the Apennines. Bogged down and frustrated, Hunt's 11th Battalion of the Eighth Army found the defences on the Aurunei and Lopini mountains impregnable. The following spring, however, the Goumiers of the French Algerian Corps, mountain men of the Atlas range, swept through the same defences *'in one murderous night.'* The allies had far too few mountain troops to make a significant difference in the Italian campaign and Lord Hunt concludes. *"It is my belief that, with more units prepared for the conditions in central Italy, to infiltrate, silent and sure-footed, in those rugged mountains and break through the crust of the German defences, Anzio would not have been necessary and the campaign might have been completed more quickly."*

In December 1943, while John Hunt was stuck below the Gustav Line, Geoffrey Rees-Jones moved the CMWTC to Cornwall to train hard in cliff assault, in preparation for D-Day. Crucial in his decision making was his idea to use small boats (dorys) to land commandos on otherwise inaccessible cliffs. He recalls that there was some opposition to this because Cornwall was in the American Zone. But, the peninsula always provided a lee-shore for training the dory-force as well as being good for climbing training. The new base for the centre was in St. Ives.

It is significant to record here that during the war the commando climbers experimented with anything and everything that would get them onto, up, and off cliffs with their wounded. Rees-Jones, himself was an extraodinary innovator and all manner of gadgetry was knocked-up in the St. Ives blacksmith's shop. Most significant was 'the grip fast' – a metal ring with big hooks attached which made a belay point on cliff tops by spreading the hooks and tapping them into the ground. Incredibly, the device also worked on sand and could anchor a 'Death Slide' rig which takes considerable loading. Rees-Jones also trained himself to route find by viewing aerial photographs of cliffs through a stereoscopic viewer. Another Rees-Jones innovation was to use his Scots contingent to get his men 'on their toes' instinctively aware that having them doing highland dancing outside the Sloop Inn, St. Ives was good for getting them climbing-fit. It was another forty years before rock climbers took 'aerobics' seriously again. No wonder Cornwall got its reputation for hard grades!

Far more horrific was the training for night-time cliff assaults in St. Ives Bay. The dories would bump against the Carrack Gladden cliffs at Hawk's Point and the climbers attempt to assault the killas cliff and steep grass above. The only option for the men who fell into the sea was to swim for Carbis Bay beach in the blackout. Day light would see the shore patrol pick up the hypothermic survivors from the night's excercise and take them to a local boiler room to warm up. Some did, some died — such were the realities of learning to climb in wartime. Modern coasteers and 'deep water' soloists may take a pause to reflect on the desperate beginnings of their sport!

Ultimately the conclusion of all these commando experiments was that the best way up a cliff was to have a good leader climb up and fix a rope for the others to climb. Climbing remained conventional, up to the point of fixing the ropes and aerial runways. The equipment and training began to evolve to assist the leader achieve his mission with a degree of safety. Most of which came from the head, becoming good at finding your line, climbing it and building supreme confidence from the principle that 'a good leader never falls'. While the climbers trained hard for the D-Day landings the dory 'Keep Force' reconnoitred the occupied coastline of France for unguarded cliffs and covert points of entry.

I have given a detailed account of the early days of the CMWTC because it originated with No 5 Commando in the South East Cornwall area. For the continuation of this climbing history after the war years I would refer readers to Des Hannigan's excellent account in The Climbers' Club West Penwith Guides. Following the war the CMWTC, which had increasingly become mixed with both Army and Royal Marine Commando units (the first marines arrived as instructors at the CMWTC in 1943), became the Royal Marine Commando Cliff Assault Wing. This unit eventually moved to Devon, but during the '40s and '50s it produced what was effectively the first corps of professional climbers in Great Britain. When these men retired from the service they continued, in various degrees to practise their skills. Some became guides, some Outward Bound instructors while others continued climbing for fun. Many stayed or returned to Cornwall having married local girls while stationed here.

The influence of the Commando Climbers on the South West scene was profound; as it was on the development of post-war mountaineering as a whole. One former commando instructor, Jim Smith, who had settled in St. Ives was responsible for teaching hundreds their initial skills: from Mike Banks (who later commanded the Cliff Assault Wing from 1955 – 58 and was the first OC to insist his men recorded their routes) to Norman Croucher, the Cornish Himalayan mountaineer who began climbing after losing both legs below the knee. Smith also trained the next group of climbers to impact on South East Cornwall, the climbers of the Truro School Rock Climbing Club.

Jim Smith, who was awarded a BEM for his work, began running rock climbing courses for youngsters during the 1950s, it had been one of these that had attracted Norman Croucher into the sport. It is probably true to say that every one who learnt to climb in Cornwall and South West Devon from 1946 to 1966 did so under the auspices of former commandos - the legacy of Geoffrey-Rees Jones. Elsewhere the ideas of Dr. Kurt Hahn and John Hunt were also being realised. Hahn had founded the Outward Bound movement, the first school opening at Aberdovey, in 1943. It was a civilian equivalent of CMWTC for many ex-commando instructors. Following the ascent of Everest, Hahn, remembering Hunt's wartime report, invited him to assist with the development of Duke of Edinburgh Award Scheme, of which Hunt became the first secretary, in 1956.

In the 1950s Commando climbing activity was focused on West Penwith, The Dewerstone and Dartmoor. The Cliff Assault Wing moved from St. Ives to Bickleigh, Devon in 1949 and although large parties where moving through Cornwall to reach West Penwith everything in South East Cornwall was again passed by with the exception of Roche which attracted the attention of D. J. Bassett who in the early 50s repeated most of the original climbs and doubtless explored a few more. In 1955, G. J. Sutton produced four climbs of which the delectable *Moping Owl* at Very Severe remains a prized gem. During the 50s Roche attracted increased attention particularly from Keith Lawder and E. C. (Ted) Pyatt who revived interest in the area. Pyatt, although not a new route bagger, was a great explorer of potential climbing areas in Cornwall and Devon during this period. His book *A Climber in the West Country* published in 1968 pointed to many a future venue. Dave Bassett too, was something of a ranger. Famous for his first ascent of *Aviation* on Hay Tor, Dartmoor he climbed at Cheesewring in its pre-climbing history, not bothering to make records, and also on the appalling loose cliffs on the Devon side of the Tamar at Gunnislake.

Schoolboys

Living in St. Ives W. A. (Toni) Carver had scrambled about the local greenstone crags since early childhood gradually, and unknown to himself, reaching a solo standard of *Severe 4b/c*. A minor fall in 1959 encouraged his parents to persuade him to seek out Jim Smith. Climbing was only a holiday activity initially until Carver, a boarder at Truro School, persuaded his friends Peter Stanier and Howard Balman, to try climbing. The three friends began to lobby hard to be allowed to start a climbers' club at the school which was not a prospect relished by the staff! However, the commando instruction gave them an edge and in December 1963 the Truro School Rock Climbing Club with nine original members was granted two weekends per term out of school for climbing meets, without any staff involvement. Jim Smith was employed by the club as their guide and instructor.

Peter Stanier's family lived in Liskeard. As a child he knew Cheesewring Quarry well from family walks in the area – seeking

Peter Stanier making a bold, early attempt on the line of Sunset Arete VS 4b in 1965. The line eventually fell to Denis Morrod in 1972.

Lords of the 'Wring. Pat Littlejohn (first left standing top) and Peter Biven (centre) reach the summit after the third ascent of Eyefull Tower E2 5a/6a, in 1967. *Photo: Rennie Gold*

Toni Carver on the first ascent of Peter V. *Diff 4a* the first route recorded at Cheesewring Quarry in August 1964.

Richard Grose pictured in the Minions Climbers' Hut where he took up permanent residence in the 1960s.

The late Peter Biven on the 5c (aided) crux of Eyefull Tower during the third ascent. *Photo: Rennie Gold*

The Minions Group was formed from members of the Truro School Rock Climbing Club and regular visitors to the Minions Climbers' Hut following the Whitsun Meet of 1969 when this photograph was taken. The photograph provided the inspiration for the group's logo.

Toni Carver rounding the arete of High Noon *E3 5c* in the days before the protection bolt was added and a ground fall was the price of failure. Carver made three ascents of the dangerous arete before the bolt.

Andrew McFarlane on the second ascent of Gather Darkness *E3 5c* which he made with Ian Rogers in August 1970. 'Mac' had also led the second ascent of High Noon earlier in the year with Carver.

John Burley and Toni Carver aiding the overhang of TDK, Hawk's Tor in the 1960s. In 1986 it went free at *6b*.

Bob Lambourne making 'another attempt' on the short lived aid climb Summer Soldier.

Dave Armitage and Steve Miles making an attempt on Super Indirect in 1973. A tough artifical route then, at *A2* - and even tougher now as a mixed climb at *E4 6a & A2*!

Dr. Peter Stanier, pioneer and discoverer of the climbing a Cheesewring. An industrial arch aeologist, successful popular autho and an expert on Cornish granite.

Cheesewring climbers spanning thirty-four years of East Cornwall's climbin history Sean Hawken, Andy Grieve and Toni Carver pictured by Tobi Carve during the production of this guidebook.

out Daniel Gumb's Euclidean carvings, moorstones and other marks of former moorlanders. These early explorations left a profound impression on his young mind and today he is one of the foremost authorities on Cornwall's industrial past and an expert on every aspect of granite, a rock he loves with an almost perverse affection! It was at his suggestion that the climbing possibilities of the quarry were to be explored.

During the heat wave of August 1964, Carver and Stanier cycled into the quarry; had it been raining Carver might never have returned! But, he was immediately struck by the lines of *Mecca* and *The Trampoline*. Stanier was horrified, he had not considered climbing on the main quarry face although he now argues that his instincts were ahead of their time – afterall the recent hard new 'sport' climbs are mostly on the smaller outcrops and it had been the Southern Outcrop that had attracted his attention! A compromise was reached and *Peter* on the eastern side of the main face was the first line to be climbed. *The Trampoline* and *Mecca* had to wait until the following year.

With the discovery of Cheesewring the Truro School Rock Climbing Club moved into top gear. Without staff supervision the club was responsible for its own good behaviour and accident free management only to the school's headmaster, D. W. Burrell. As patron of the club Derek Burrell sponsored the first term-time meet at Minions when the club stayed in the Cheesewring Hotel. "With our gear strung all over the stairs and banisters the place looked more like the Wasdale Head in 1890 than Cornwall in the Swinging 60s" Carver recalled later: "The gear was about the same vintage too!" It was a situation that could not continue so Derek Burrell began negotiations to lease the former Minions Working Men's Institute from the Duchy of Cornwall.

It is perhaps not without interest that the Duchy were well disposed to assisting with youth development during the period. The Minions Institute had been rented out to a local farmer as a barn with the proviso that he would be willing to surrender it should it be required for community activity and the club fitted the bill. Gordonstoun's extraodinary headmaster, Kurt Hahn, responsible both for the education of Prince Philip and the originator of the Duke of Edinburgh's Award Scheme had set a mood which greatly assisted the TSRCC. Prince Charles, Duke of Cornwall, was also a Gordonstoun man.

The technical developments introduced into climbing during the commando years included laid nylon rope which replaced hemp. Stiff rubber, cleated 'vibram' soled service boots which, following the war, replaced tricouni nailed boots; and 'dynamic' belaying – a more careful technique of body belaying. Almost all climbing gear available in the '40s and '50s was ex-war department and very heavy. During the '60s at Cheesewring the footwear changed from big boots, through lighter klettershues to modern rock boots, although the quality of the rubber did not approach today's standard until the mid-1980s. By 1967 a variety of thin, small hard steel pitons were available from the United States which provided marginally better protection on the harder climbs. However, the first nuts were useless at Cheesewring and not until the advent of the smaller 'friends' and micro nuts did it become possible, to some degree, to replicate the standards of protection available on natural cliffs and outcrops.

Commando trained, the Truro Club grossly underestimated their abilities which is reflected in the grades. *The Trampoline*, for example, originally graded at *Very Difficult*, is now at a more realistic *Hard Very Severe 4c (PP)* but it remains as dangerous as ever! With Carver's ascents of 1967, *Eyefull Tower, High Noon* and *Silva Gray*, climbing standards at Cheesewring matched those everywhere else in the South West but the climbs were rather more dangerous. A characteristic which was not missed by Peter Biven who with the young Pat Littlejohn made the third ascent of *Eyefull Tower* on 29th of May 1967.

Biven, who found Cheesewring *'a serious crag'* and *Eyefull Tower, 'strenuous and delicate also'* commented that there was *'not much protection on the upper section.'* His suggestion was that bolts would be an appropriate form of protection in the quarry. Carver was originally reluctant to follow this advice, knowing of Biven's disquiet over his own use of bolts on *Beowulf* at Bosigran the previous year. The Cheesewring ascents had been made without the 'bomb proof' security provided by bolts. However, others too voiced their support for the idea notably the outstanding Plymouth climber Len Benstead, a strong and bold leader, who made a failed attempt at the second ascent of *High*

Noon, quite understandably. At this time a leader falling from the *5b* mantleshelf on *High Noon* had the same distance between himself and the first belay as his second had between the stance and the ground with no intermediate runners possible. Such a risk was clearly unjustifiable for visitors so in 1969, with some reluctance, Carver added a bolt to *Eyefull Tower* and one to the 'terminal' second pitch of *High Noon*.

On *High Noon*, Carver had been partnered by his frequent companion on the harder climbs, Richard Grose. The day before the first ascent Grose had belayed on a marginal peg in the corner next to the mantleshelf. "He knew that if the peg had to take the strain of a fall it would pull," Carver said later. "If I had fallen I would have catapulted him into oblivion but I knew he would slow me down and save me before leaving!" The pair climbed to below the last pitch on that first day but on the next, the first ascent proper, Carver was not prepared to risk his second above the first belay which: "In view of the previous day this seemed only fair!" Perhaps it is not suprising that Richard Grose's father, who had always encouraged his son's climbing, had served with 5 Commando during the war.

With free climbing now seemingly at the edge of what was possible – nearly two decades were to elapse before Nick Hancock, Ken Palmer and Andy Grieve began their campaign to eliminate aid points – the attractions of the quarry for artificial climbing became obvious. In July '67 Trevor Newberry and Trevor Benjamin were first to climb Fortress Wall with *Expensive A2*, the first artificial climb on the main face at Cheesewring. Twenty-one years later a more direct variation of the line, *Special Offer* was climbed free at *E3 6a*.

A cluster of easier climbs discovered in '69, including Stanier's *The Purple Revrac* and Carver's *Star Fox*, became popular overnight and remained so. Plymouth climbers Mike Bradford and Dennis Morrod broke the incestuous hold of the locals with their ascent of *Bird Line*. 1970 saw a determined assault on the big artificial lines by an outstanding group of Plymouth climbers including Len Benstead who, partnered by Morrod, produced *Khyber Wall* A1 (now free) and the dramatic *Black Panther* A3 which still awaits a free ascent in its entirety. Benstead also produced *Warrior* (now free) with Steve Chadwick who bagged the lead on *Super Indirect*. Other Plymouth climbers, Barry

Hocken and Ian Rogers, climbed *Spectral Radius* and Andrew McFarlane made the second ascent of *High Noon* seconded by its originator. In October Chadwick and McFarlane climbed *Black Sabbath* A3 of which much has now gone free but the headwall still remains as a last great challenge for today's activists.

The 1970's were a quiet period for development at Cheesewring and South East Cornwall as a whole which is not to say that it was not a busy decade. The TSRCC Hut, which had provided such a firm base for the initial developments, continued to bustle with regular activity as The Minions Group, an adventure club formed from the Cheesewring regulars, continued exploring the Moor. There were mines to descend, walks to be enjoyed, canoeing techniques to be learnt in the Gold Diggings ponds, parties on the Cheesewring, and books to be written.

The first of these was *Climbing in Cornwall* by Carver, Stanier and Pat Littlejohn. With his ascents at Tintagel, Pentire and Carn Gowla on the north Cornwall coast Littlejohn had become the dominant force in South West climbing and the three writers had identified a need for a guide which covered the rest of Cornwall outside West Penwith of which this was to be the first. During the course of checking for the guide the climbing at Dodman Point was discovered and Carver produced *Prince Heathen*. Later this prompted a visit from Littlejohn resulting in the aptly named *Horrorshow* E4 6a.

Any hope that this dramatic route would signify the beginning of a period of the intense, high standard development (Littlejohn's hallmark) on this coast proved to be tragically short lived. In 1975, while exploring Nare Head with his long standing partner Keith Darbyshire, Darbyshire fell into the sea and was killed. The mid-seventies were not a happy period for Cornish climbers in this respect as the deaths of other leading figures; Peter Biven, Alison Chadwick, Mark Dawson and Frank Harvey drew a particularly golden age to a close.

Climbing in Cornwall was reviewed by BBC TV's *Spotlight* programme which featured an ascent of *Eyefull Tower* by Carver and Stanier. For this ascent a second bolt was added to 'back-up' the original, considered to be getting old after four years. The two bolts on this climb are still the originals so caution is advised! The publication in 1973 of the guide came too soon to catch Steve

Chadwick's last bold contribution to Cheesewring *One Way Ticket E2* 5b which was a precursor to the later hard developments on the Western Outcrop and which was unseconded. In 1976 after being 'suitably impressed' with *One Way Ticket*, Tim Mason climbing with Minions Group member, Bob Lambourne, produced the excellent *Second Class Return*. The pair also added some lines to that most traditional of the area's crags, The Devil's Jump. Mason and Lambourne also produced *Porky* at Roche in the early 1970s, a fine little climb, which fell victim to the prevailing attitude of the day which considered it unnecessary to publish descriptions of obvious lines on the easier crags. Roche and Hawk's Tor received only generalised descriptions in the 1973 guide which was something of a disservice to less able climbers and beginners. Roche at this time had become a 'solo anywhere' venue for the area's harder climbers particularly Rob Walker and Bob Bennett neither of whom where inclined to record their activities there.

Around this time Carver made repeated attempts at free climbing the line of *Trouble With Lichen E3 6a* on the Western Outcrop determined to resist aid. His frequent failures were, he pathetically claims, because: "My boots just kept sliding off at the crux!" The history of this little route provides a bridge between the new and the old at Cheesewring as the line eventually fell in Feb '75 as the aid climb *Summer Soldier* to Martin Dunning climbing with Tim Mason. Its subsequent free ascent and renaming by Andy Grieve in 1985 was to mark the commencement of the current wave of development in South East Cornwall which heralded a decade of considerable physical achievement.

In 1981 the management of the Minion's Climbers Hut reverted to Truro School who now use it as an outdoor education centre. The loss of the facility to the wider climbing community was softened somewhat when 'quarrying' of the massive blocks in the waste tips in and around Cheesewring Quarry commenced in 1984. This changed the topography of the quarry considerably, leaving it even more exposed to easterly winds, but without damaging any of the climbing faces. The Minions Group held its last official meet at the hut over the New Year of 1980/81 when their curious tradition of seeing the New Year in from the top of the Cheesewring was last observed.

Toni Carver on pitch two of *Silva Gray* during the 1960s

HISTORY NOTES – MODERN

Sean Hawken

ALL NEW ROUTING in South East Cornwall ceased, with not a single climb recorded between the spring of 1976 and the autumn of 1984. At the Cheesewring Quarry large amounts of granite stock piles were removed for road building, happily the rock faces suffered no ill effect from the operations.

In the mid 1980s a new character entered the game of climbing new routes. Andy Grieve arrived on the scene and set about making the area a much more attractive climbing venue. He may be short in stature (only jesting), but nevertheless what he lacks in size he makes up for in ability. Within the borders of South East Cornwall he has accomplished more first ascents than any other climber.

Grieve teamed up with his friends, Ken Palmer whom he had met whilst working in the dockyard and Nick Hancock who had been a member of the old Kernow Climbing Club. Following the rest of the country's lead, they arrived at the Cheesewring Quarry with the intention of eliminating all the remaining aid points on existing climbs and free climbing the old artificial (A-graded) routes. During 1985 Grieve, made the first kill with his free ascent of the popular aid climb *Summer Soldier*, which he renamed *Trouble with Lichen*, E3 6a. Hancock, followed this by freeing the *A1* top pitch on the snaking line of *Bird Line*, E2 5c, and eliminated the aid on *Eyefull Tower*, E2 6a. Hancock's freeing of the technical crux of *Eyefull Tower* and Grieve's thin crux on *Trouble with Lichen* were impressive technically, but a more committing display of skill and mettle by Hancock came with his bold adventures up the blank line of *Dead Exit, E4* 6a. *Trouble with Lichen* (as *Summer Soldier*) and *Eyefull Tower* were already well established and popular climbs that had set the standard within the South East of Cornwall during the "Carver years", Now, with the removal of the last of their aid points these same routes were again in the vanguard for displaying the new level of commitment required to keep pace with the once again increasing technical standard.

A climb that really was to mark the new level of technical achievement developing in South East Cornwall was soon to be completed at the Cheesewring Quarry. As the three continued to climb new routes together they adopted a system of three goes or falls and you're off! At the time they were all relatively equal in ability and the system worked well, though later it was to prove a pretty harsh discipline as Grieve's efforts in cleaning and equipping the quarry's latest test piece *Agent Provocateur, E4 6b* went unrewarded and the rapidly improving Palmer notched up another first prize. 1986, was to be a fruitful year for these three, as they wandered freely tallying up their ever increasing level of first ascents.

Staying with the mid-eighties, but leaving the Cheesewring Quarry; Grieve and Hancock's visit to Nare Head on the south coast was rewarded with *Inner Secrets, E1 5b* found at the back of the small zawn and the outstanding *Moonshadow, E4 5c* further along the cliff. Grieve along with Palmer could also be found at the quarry on Kit Hill, where with the exception *Kit Hill Killer E2 6a,* the result of a visit by Pete O'Sullivan in 1984, they found the quarry devoid of climbs. Grieve's main contribution was a fine quality crack climb, *Purple Haze E2 5b.* Palmer added *A Whole Lotta Shakin' Goin' On, E3 6a* on the main slab. Quarries at this time, were not generally considered very good for free climbing and the concept of bolting was at this point not even being given breathing space. This meant that there was only a limited increase in the number of new climbs created in the quarries.

A further visit to Nare Head by Grieve and Hancock was to see them undertake a journey up what sounds a most inviting dark and damp crack, fittingly named *Dark Entries, E4 6a.* The quarry at Gold Diggings also became a target for a Grieve visit. This time, however, it was in the company of the audacious Chris Rees. They left a calling card in the form of a handful of *E2s - Mirror Mirror, E2 5b; Hamamelis E2 5c* and *Barbecue Wood, E2 5b.* 1986 finished with one more visit to Dodman Point where the stability of the rock is always questionable. Still, Hancock scratched up a photogenic *Jood the Zood, E3 5b* whilst Grieve could be found *Splitting Images* at *E2 5c,* on the upper slab.

Nationally, technical grades were rapidly rising, giving the impression that the new younger climbers were willing to undertake challenges that the 'old timers', considered beyond their grasp, however, it wasn't quite that simple. There was the vast improvement in climbing equipment to consider and substantial changes in attitude. Carver says that at the end of the 1960s and the beginning of the 1970s, "*6a*" was generally accepted as the upper limit of physical climbing ability as climbers were universally

Ken Palmer on Dark Entries (E4 6a) Nare Head.   *Photo: Nick Hancock*

Nick Hancock on Rampage (F7b) Cheesewring Quarry.   Photo: *Sean Hawken*

pursuing the *on-sight* ethic. He says: "I think each generation pushes the standards about as far as the technology will allow without taking suicidal risks, although you generally do as you near your peak!"

Without a doubt, the arrival of chalk and sticky rubber rock boots extended the possibilities for this new generation of climbers, while making existing climbs easier and less committing. Paradoxically, this lead to an upward re-evaluation of grading rather than a downward one! Along with these improvements came the arrival of more advanced protection methods, harnesses, nuts, belay devices, and of course the modern high-tech dynamic rope. As for Ray Jardine's brilliant invention of *Friends*, this was more than an innovation it was a major breakthrough! All these improvements revolutionized climbing world-wide and South East Cornwall was no exception. Now, the adage 'a good leader never falls', could, to a certain extent be dispensed with, and new limits could again be attained. Helpful as all this new technology was, however, it was a determined attitude towards practising, preparation and training, with a whole new commitment to hard physical effort, that set the new generation apart from the old.

1988 was to see Grieve make the first free ascent of the old artificial climb *Warrior, E3 5c* at the Cheesewring Quarry, utilising the old bolt heads and thin knife blades for protection (due to the poor quality of the old bolts this route has undergone a face lift and now it is protected with new bolts and stainless steel pegs). Steve Mayers arrived at the quarry later in the year. He successfully set the highest standards of the time, in the area, with his ascents of *Psycokiller, E6 6c* and *Wring the Changes, E6 6c*. Indeed! At the time of writing, *Psycokiller* could still be the hardest climb here as it still awaits a successful second ascent. Mayers also accidentally claimed *Warrior* and *Special Offer, E3 6a*, both of which Grieve had completed earlier in the year.

There were two major differences between Mayers' routes and those of Grieve, Palmer and Hancock. Mayers' routes were not only physically more demanding than anything else previously climbed in South East Cornwall, they were also protected by new bolts. This was not the first time the quarry had resounded to the sound of hammer and drill, for bolts have long been accepted in Cheesewring Quarry. The earliest examples are from the 1960s and can be found at former aid points and on old artificial climbs. Many of these old bolts have corroded away or been replaced for protection where the climbs have changed to free routes. Mayers did not stay long, he left again in the same year, leaving Grieve, Palmer and Hancock wondering if their approach to climbing hadn't already become out dated. Palmer changed tack and followed Mayers' example on the main central wall of the quarry, where he produced the superb line of *Mauritius, E5 6b/c*.

At the end of the decade young Lee Earnshaw, lost and lonely, wandered all the way down from Plymouth in search of new interests and found himself where else to start, but the Cheesewring Quarry! 1989 saw Earnshaw notch up a handful of mid-grade routes in the quarry. His best contribution alluded him until 1991, when he freed the old aid route of *Rene, E4 6a* using old rusty tied-off bolt heads in the same style as Grieve on *Warrior* (*Rene* has also undergone a face lift and now sports two 10mm bolts). Earnshaw could also be found doing his, "Doctor Livingstone impression" within the swamps and dense foliage of Luxulyan Valley. He along with his friend Dave Gillard managed to produce several jungle style routes, such as *Drippy & Strangely Brown, HVS 5a*.

During the early 1990s the adventurous Chris Rees produced two superb, but terrifying new lines at Dodman Point, the first was the curiously named *Sex Tips For Monogamous Girls, E3 5b* and the second route, the only climb in the area to be graded *XS - Exceptionally Severe*, the aptly named *Dod on Arrival, XS 5b*. The stylish classic of *Special Llama, E5 6a* at Kilmar Tor, was to be Palmer's final piece of work in South East Cornwall. Palmer moved on to pastures new in Devon, were he started a very successful campaign of hard training and commitment at Anstey's Cove — "Forget not your routes Ken."

1991 was to see Dave Turnbull beat Grieve in a little friendly competition for the first ascent of *On Mirkwood Edge, E4 6b*, in the Lost World Quarry at Luxulyan. Rees, back looking for adventure and again in the company of Grieve, climbed the Treffry Viaduct at Luxulyan. Later, he was to be seen, in a moment of madness swimming the length of the viaduct, creating this guidebook's only swim *Captain Webb* (included for fun and not recommended).

A new team formed early in 1991 as Sean Hawken, a local lad, joined the unstoppable Grieve in producing a new collection of first ascents. Grieve found a line right of *Agent Provocateur* giving the sport climb *Double Agent, F7a (E4 6a)*. After much discussion over control and containment, Hawken started a new regime of controlled bolting at the Cheesewring Quarry. The first line to fall was *Potential Energy, F6c+ (E3 6a)*, a worthwhile line up the left side of the Western Outcrop wall (*Double Agent* was then re-climbed using the start of this route, producing one of the Quarry's best routes). All the bolting was undertaken using a hand drill to ensure a minimalist impact programme. It was decided that the new bolted sports routes should only be produced, as long as they had no effect on the standing traditional lines and this policy is still in use today. Seeing the achievements of Mayers and Palmer, the advantages of the new style 'sport climbing' now became apparent to the traditionally minded Andy Grieve. Realising the potential of Cheesewring Quarry as a sport climbing venue he accepted the inevitable changes and decided to join in.

1993 continued to be a good year for Grieve and Hawken with a new young aspirant Caroline Carpenter in a supporting role, they worked on in the quarry producing an array of fine climbs. Hawken's next project was a fine looking route on the arete right of *Khyber Wall*, he called it *Khyber Pass, E4 6a*. At the time, working strictly to the minimal bolting policy, he perhaps sadly opted to use only three bolts and the result was a fine looking climb that is a little awkward to assess, as it is neither a true sport climb, nor a traditional climb in the accepted customary sense.

With a degree of apprehension that maybe he was going against his long standing beliefs, Grieve set about producing his first bolted sport route. The result however, was *Real Live Wire, F7b (E5 6b)* an inspiring, quality climb running up the central wall of the main overhang, finishing at a junction with Mayers' *Psychokiller* and *Wring the Changes*. This was followed by the classic *Rampage,* at *F7b (E5 6b)*. Watching Grieve make the first ascent of this route was very entertaining, as at the time he was a bolt hanger short for the three bolts on the ramp section. Instead of waiting a couple of days, he decided to climb up and out, clipping the first two bolts, before climbing back to his original high stance at the first bolt. This in itself was a superb effort, as the ramp is solid *6a*, from start to finish. From his lofty perch on the stance, he was able to remove the first bolt hanger and once more ascended the raising ramp. This time though on arriving at the third bolt placement, he had to hang on with one hand, whilst he screwed the bolt hanger on with the other hand and all before being able to safely clip in. Once he had completed the task and could precariously rest at the end of the ramp he commented, ironically, that clipping gear on sports climbs, was harder than placing fiddly RP's.

1994 saw Grieve knock off the thought provoking line of *Friend or Foe F7a+ (E4 6b)*, whilst Hawken worked on the short, but power packed *Tag F7b (E5 6b)* and the strenuous line of *Cosmic Joker F7b (E5 6b)*. Earnshaw made another brief visit, producing the very popular *Feline Adventures F6b (E2 5c)*. In June 1995, Hawken provided the Cheesewring Quarry with more stony test pieces, first came the interesting *Crucifier F7a (E4 6a)*, which was quickly followed by the creative fingery *Sweet Surrender F7c (E6 6b/c)*. Grieve was hot on his trail with the intricately thin slab of *Le Tour, F7a+ (E4 6b)* and the fiery *Hot Lava, F7c (E6 6c)*.

Grieve and Hawken moved down to Roche Rock for a break from sports climbing. Here very much in traditional style, Grieve led the way up the finger crack in the main overhang to produce a gritstone style classic *God Forbid, E4 6b* (named after reading the sign informing the public of no climbing on the monastery).

The work of Grieve and Hawken has ensured that the new sports routes have rapidly filled in the last of the gaps at Cheesewring and have caused a revival of interest, as the quarry has swiftly become a very popular venue for visiting climbers. The Plymouth crowd in particular seemed delighted with the change, fully appreciating the chance to stretch out, without encountering the usual Cheesewring horror trips. Today the quarry offers a wide choice of new and old styled routes to suit all tastes, from *Diff* to *E6*, or if you prefer from *F6a* up to *F7c*.

The Cheesewring Quarry is not the only new or revived venue. In 1995 Gold Diggings received its hardest test piece to date: *The Darkness Beckons, F7a+ (E4 6b)* with the compliments of Grieve. Hawk's Tor received a visit from Hawken accompanied by Tim Catterall. They left a good handful of short challenging climbs, that have a great similarity to climbing on the Tors of Dartmoor. Malcolm Rescorle's *Just Good Friends, VS 5a* at Trewartha Tor, is one of those lonely gems that deserves a visit, as does Hawken's *Sleepy Hollow, E1 5b* on Kilmar Tor.

Helman Tor is a wonderful bouldering venue that had received much bouldering effort from others in the past but with little or no documentation. Grieve, Hawken, Hancock and Rescorle all put effort into working and documenting old and exciting new boulder problems for the delectation of avid bouldering fans. Whilst bouldering at Helman Tor, Hawken found *Bloody Helman* an *E4 6a* and named it after a comment that followed a fall which resulted in a chipped tooth.

New routing continued in (and very near) this South East Cornwall guidebook area in 1996, prior to the guide's completion. *Divine Comedy, E1 5a* was produced by Hawken crossing the large loose break on the upper cliff at Dodman Point. The efforts of Carver's sons did not go unnoticed as they began cutting their own path in the new route game. Barnaby Carver spotted a long overlooked, but surprisingly obvious line at the Cheesewring Quarry which he pointed his elder brother, Tobi, at — creating *Heart of Darkness, E2 5b* in the traditional style. However, by the summer the Carvers had moved back west, across the Fal to develop the other Black Head, the one near Coverack.

Coastal locations also became attractive to Hancock, Catterall, Grieve and Hawken as they began to investigate the possibilities of 'deep water soloing' at Pencarrow Head producing a number of climbs in the genre, including; *The Go Between, HVS 5a* and *Grim Reefer, E1 5b*. Pencarrow also produced a full blown route *Rubble Without a Cause, E4 5c*. Grieve and Hawken continued to develop tough routes throughout the year adding a *6b* top pitch to *Hot Lava* and producing *Double Trouble, E3 6a* and *Pooh Pooh, E3 5b* at Cheesewring while at Luxulyan Quarry they produced *Strongbow* a three star *F7c*. The pair also began to exploit the summit rocks of Rough Tor and found *Chicken in the Rough, E5 6b*, a discovery that might bode well for some of the moor's long neglected tors. The year finished with the completion of Grieve and Hawken's long term project at Cheesewring '*Our Carver*', *F7c* a major contribution to the crag in the modern mode of sport climbing.

As to the future of rock climbing in South East Cornwall. It can be said without doubt that as far as new routes are concerned we will see very little further development in the Cheesewring Quarry, as nearly all the lines have now been completed. There is, however, still scope for a handful of high grade extreme sports routes (*F8a* and above). The Tors of Bodmin moor could be further worked, resulting in perhaps a good handful of arduous short problematic routes and boulder problems. The South Coast has always been an acquired taste because there is always the problem of poor rock quality. However, this may change as South East Cornwall becomes further developed and the coast continues to offer a haven for those seeking adventure and freedom far from the madding crowds. Good luck to all those involved and to all those who make an effort to repeat these routes.

KIT HILL QUARRY

This quarry has not seen any real development since the last guidebook by Iain Peters. The routes are up to 50ft high and the base of the quarry is filled with water, although it is possible to get most of the way around the base, via a system of rock hopping.

HOW TO FIND

From Callington drive towards Tavistock (A390); before St. Anne's Chapel turn left to Luckett and left again within one mile. This track will take you to the top of Kit Hill, the quarry is down the short track on the right.

THE CLIMBS

The climbs are on your right as you enter the Quarry, running right to left. There are some easier climbs that see regular ascents but have never been recorded - enjoy!

(1) **A Whole Lotta Shakin' Goin' On** 40ft *E3 6a (AP)* ★1986
Climb the largest slab past three peg runners.

(2) **Chocolate Orange** 45ft *E2 5b (PP)* 1986
Climb the orange slab left of *A Whole Lot of Shakin' Goin' On* with two peg runners (not in place).

(3) **Kit Hill Killer** 45ft *E2 6a (AP)* 1984
At the back of the quarry there is a clean face. Climb the very thin crack on the right side of the face to the left of an obvious jamming crack, past a peg runner, to a ledge. Continue up a shallow corner finishing via the arete.

(4) **Purple Haze** 50ft *E2 5b (AP)* ★★1986
A great route. Start 5ft left of the line of *Kit Hill Killer*, and climb a left trending series of holds up the wall. Two peg runners.

(5) **True Grit** 30ft *E2 5b (AP)* 1987
A poor climb that takes the tapering crack on the opposite side of the quarry to *Purple Haze*.

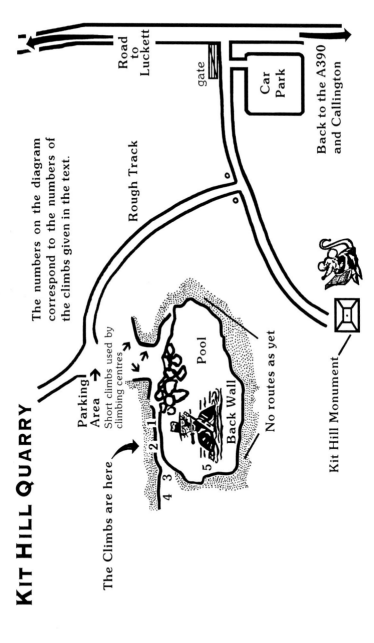

KIT HILL QUARRY

The numbers on the diagram correspond to the numbers of the climbs given in the text.

The Climbs are here

Parking Area

Short climbs used by climbing centres

Rough Track

Road to Luckett

gate

Car Park

Back to the A390 and Callington

Pool

Back Wall

No routes as yet

Kit Hill Monument

60

Sean Hawken on Agent Provocateur (E4 6b) Cheesewring Quarry.   *Photo: Andy Grieve*

Tobi Carver on Heart of Darkness (E2 5b) Cheesewring Quarry. *Photo: Toni Carver*

CHEESEWRING QUARRY
MAIN FACE & WESTERN OUTCROP

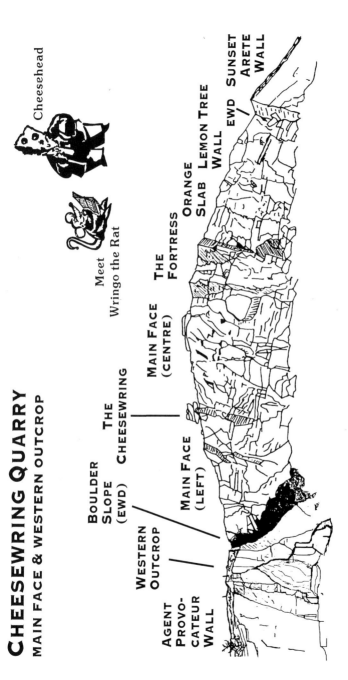

Cheesehead

Meet
Wringo the Rat

AGENT PROVO-
CATEUR
WALL

WESTERN
OUTCROP

MAIN FACE
(LEFT)

BOULDER
SLOPE
(EWD)

THE
CHEESEWRING

MAIN FACE
(CENTRE)

THE
FORTRESS

ORANGE
SLAB

LEMON TREE
WALL

EWD

SUNSET
ARETE
WALL

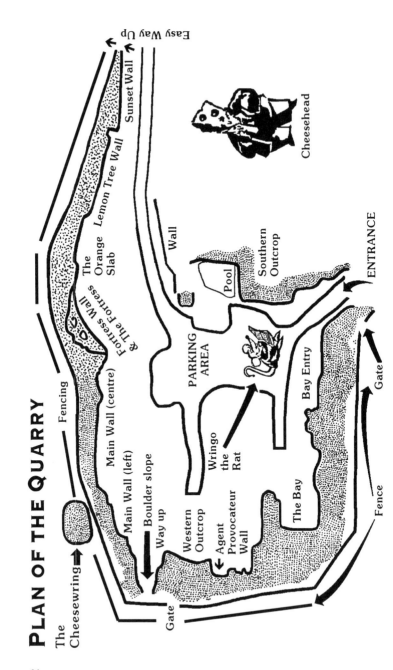

PLAN OF THE QUARRY

The Cheesewring

Fencing

Main Wall (left)

Main Wall (centre)

Boulder slope

Way up

Fortress Wall & The Fortress

The Orange Slab

Lemon Tree Wall

Sunset Wall

Easy Way Up

Western Outcrop

Agent Provocateur Wall

Gate

Wringo the Rat

PARKING AREA

The Bay

Bay Entry

Wall

Pool

Southern Outcrop

ENTRANCE

Gate

Fence

Cheesehead

64

THE CHEESEWRING QUARRY

Landranger, OS sheet 201 GR 256729

The Cheesewring quarry is situated on the southern side of Stowes Hill, near the village of Minions, about four miles north of Liskeard. The premier crag of the area, Cheesewring has much to offer with climbing of all grades from Moderate up to, and including, E6. There is now a wider selection of hard sport climbs, with the Western Outcrop holding some of the best steep fingery challenges. *Double Agent* is typical whilst on both flanks of this wall; *Tag*, *Sweet Surrender* and *Feline Adventures* offer overhanging pump. Over in the Central Bay longer hard routes like *Psychokiller* and the superb *Mauritius* can be found. With the traditional style still very much in evidence you may like to try routes such as the '67 challenge of *Simanon Direct* (left side, main face) or the newer *Bored of the Wrings* (left, main face). Beginners may like to start on the short Southern Outcrop where top ropes can easily be set up and, with an easy walk off the back, it lends itself to safer lessons.

The rock changes character throughout the quarry, but is generally of compact granite, which in places tends to be smooth and in the wet can prove to be very slippery. The encircling rock gives the appearance of an amphitheatre and on entry can appear sombre and uninviting especially in winter, but hang around and you'll find that with a little sunshine it warms up. This is due to the surrounding walls holding the heat in and keeping the wind out. In an attempt to dispel any reputation of only dangerous unprotected climbing, several of the older pegs have been replaced and many of the new climbs have been bolted. There is a wide consensus over the appropriate use of bolts among climbers active in South East Cornwall but visitors should be aware that local policy is quite close to that of the BMC and even in quarries careful consideration should be given to each new placement (see introduction). Cheesewring Quarry is owned by the Duchy of Cornwall who have never objected to climbing here. Although not commonly practised, permission to climb should be obtained from the Duchy on: 01579 343194.

HOW TO FIND

Minions village can be reached by travelling north from Liskeard through the village of St. Cleer, but perhaps the easiest approach is now from Doublebois on the A38, between Liskeard and Bodmin. Here, a turn at a well signposted cross-roads leads north-east, past Common Moor, to Minions (approximately five and a half miles). Beyond the village on the left, a rough dirt track leads past a converted mine engine house, now the Minions Area Information Centre to the quarry. There is a car park on the right and the quarry is about half a mile further along the track at its end.

THE SOUTHERN OUTCROP

This thirty foot high outcrop, which is situated immediately on the right as one enters the quarry, has traditionally been regarded as a practice crag offering a variety of short routes in the lower grades. It has easy access to the top via a simple scramble at the entrance, and with a flat top and good belays, it's a great place to teach beginners. The most obvious feature on this face is the small corner in the centre, this being *Central Corner*.

THE CLIMBS

The climbs are described left to right.

(1) **Left Arete**   20ft   *Severe 4b (WP)*   1960s
The left hand arete is climbed on its left side via a large crack until near the top then turn the arete on it's right side to finish.

(2) **Learner Route**   25ft   *Difficult 3b (AP)*   1960s
Climb onto the first ledge and then using the right side corner gain the next large ledge, move right again to finish up the stepped right hand corner.

(3) **Variation Start**   20ft *Very Difficult 4b (AP)* ★1960s
Climb directly up to the right side of the ledge via a small layback fault, to a large standing ledge. Then to finish, step left and continue up the smaller horizontal breaks on the face.

(4) **Moss Trap**   25ft   *E1 5a (NP)*   1989
The mossy wall just to the right of the last route has been climbed finishing right on loose holds. Very eliminate and covered in moss

(5) **Half Route Half Boulder Problem** 25ft *E3 5c (NP)* 1987
The centre of the blank wall is taken via small holds and extremely bold climbing. Move up to and over the overhangs continually trending right.

(6) **Central Corner** 30ft *Hard Very Severe 5b (AP)* ★★1960s/71
Climb the shallow corner past an old rusty peg (back it up). To finish break right out of the top of the crack and carry on up the face above.

Editor's Note: When Len Benstead eliminated the last point of aid on this popular 60's aid route he renamed it *Pink Panther* but the new name never stuck, probably because the climb was already well known.

(7) **Debutante**   25ft   *E3 6a (AP)*   ★1993
The face of the wall right of Central Corner. The face can be climbed via a difficult sequence of moves, past a peg runner. Follow the thin cracks to the top.

(8) **Corner Seat**   25ft   *Hard Severe 4b (PP)*   1960s
Climb the stepped inside corner right of Debutante.

(9) **The Garden Gate** 25ft *Hard Very Severe 5a (AP)* ★1960s
A good climb. Take the right side of the corner to a height of about 4ft. Move out right onto the face using very small holds. Then reach up high to gain larger holds. Climb up then move back left to finish through the overhang on good holds.

(10) **Garden Wall**   25ft   *Hard Severe 4c (AP)*   1960s
Six feet right of the corner there is an easier break which traverses left to the small hanging arete, use this and then finish using the arete on its right hand side.

(11) **Right Arete**   *30ft Hard Severe 4b (PP)*   1960s
The right arete of the wall is climbed moving left near the top on loose holds.

Bay Entry

On the left as one enters the quarry is a short steep wall. The most prominent feature being the short diagonally lying arete.

THE CLIMBS

The climbs are described from left to right.

(12) **Chocolate Hobnob** *20ft Hard Very Severe 5a (NP)* 1990

The first obvious feature on this face is a brown patch of rock. Climb awkwardly, passing some loose rock, to the top.

(13) **Half Man Half Biscuit** 25ft *E3 6a (PP)* 1986

The diagonal crack in the centre of the wall is followed to a peg runner (missing) and hard moves right gain better holds to the top.

(14) **Dwarf's Dream** 25ft *E1 5c* (AP) 1990

The often wet inside corner of the arete on the right hand side of the wall is climbed to a ledge and thin crack above. The first section can also be used as a boulder problem with an easy way down 15ft right.

(15) **Snatch** 25ft *Hard Very Severe 5b (AP)* 1994

30ft right of *Dwarf's Dream* is a short but overhanging wall which can be surmounted via a broken corner and crack above, stainless steel peg insitu, finishing right of the large block above.

Further along this wall, one comes to a dark bay which in winter can often be wet. You will now find several testing climbs here.

The Bay

THE CLIMBS

The climbs are described from left to right, starting in the left-hand corner.

(16) **Fingerbob** 25ft *E2 5c (WP)* 1992

The left hand corner of the bay moving slightly right into the wide horizontal crack (peg runner on the left wall). Climb on up the very thin crack and borehole.

BAY ENTRY

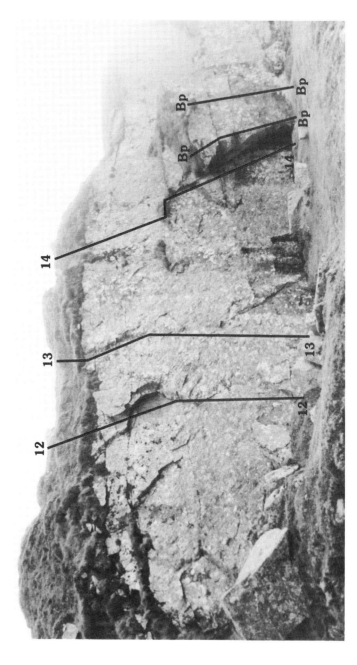

Agent Provocateur Wall

(17) **Watchman**   30ft   *E3 5c (PP)*   1994
Climb the groove in the centre of the short wall to clip a vertical knifeblade (which offers only marginal protection), move up to clip a second peg. Finish directly.

(18) **Crucifier**   45ft   *F7a (E4 6a) (WP)*   ★1995
The left-hand side of the larger section of wall, can be climbed directly to a large break.   Move on up onto the headwall staying on the right of the short arete to finish with greater difficulty.

(18a) **Pooh Pooh**   45ft   *E3 5b (AP)*   1996
Climb the obvious small corner direct. The rock quality deteriorates at three quarters height.

(19) **Cosmic Joker**   45ft   *F7b (E5 6b) (WP)*   ★1994
Takes the highest overhanging part of the wall. Start below the groove and climb up to clip the first bolt. Step right *below the second bolt, then* climb directly up the steepest part of the wall to the third bolt and a stainless steel peg. Continue to the top - a good workout.

(20) **Sheep Shit Shooter**   *35ft E3 6a (PP)*   1990
The right hand corner is taken on some loose and dirty rock. (pegs removed after first ascent).

(21) **Sidekick**   30ft   *Very Severe 5a (AP)*   1994
Climb the wide but short crack which is harder than it looks. Finish up the grassy boulders above.

THE WESTERN OUTCROP (LEFT SIDE)
The far back left corner has a short overhanging green stained wall, facing the main wall.

THE CLIMBS
The climbs are described from left to right. Starting with the short arete itself.

(22) **Rabbit Arete**   25ft   *Very Severe 4c (WP)*   1993
The arete furthest left, 40ft to the left of the Agent Provocateur wall is taken from the ground up a vertical crack and

onto a large ledge, move up past a peg runner, turning the arete on the right to finish.

(23) **Feline Adventures** 25ft *F6b (E2 5c) (WP)* ★1994
A harder variation to Rabbit Arete. Start at the same point as *Rabbit Arete* climb to the ledge but instead of surmounting the ledge, hand traverse right following the two bolts out and up the overhanging wall, finish directly.

(24) **Daisy's Flapjack** 25ft *E1 5b (AP)* 1995
Climb the inside corner directly, peg insitu at half height.

(25) **Foxglove Arete** 25ft *Very Difficult 4b (PP)* 1993
The next short broken arete 20ft feet right of *Daisy's Flapjack*.

(26) **Volker's Visit** 25ft *Severe 4b (PP)* 1993
The right-hand side of the broken arete has a shallow groove. Climb the groove to the ledge, step left and finish up the vegetated corner.

AGENT PROVOCATEUR WALL

This next small section of steep yellow speckled wall has some of the best short, but steep climbing on offer in the quarry. The sun warms this corner in the mornings even on some of the coldest winter days.

THE CLIMBS

The climbs are described from left to right.

(27) **West Point** 35ft *F6b+ (E2 6a) (AP)* 1995
Boulder up to the right of the broken arete, which is situated at the left end of the face. Move up and clip a bolt before making strenuous moves right and then up the face (insitu peg site: fixed peg was stolen in May '97) to easier but bolder climbing above.

(28) **Potential Energy** 40ft *F6c+ (E3 6a) (AP)* ★★1993
Climb directly to the bolt on the speckled wall. Move to the horizontal break, clip the peg runner of *Agent Provocateur*. Continue up to the next break move left to gain the finish via a mantel.

(29) **Double Agent**   45ft   *F7a (E4 6a) (AP)* ★★★1993
Start as for *Potential Energy*, traverse right at the first horizontal break. Now move up on spaced holds, small friend peg
runners, to finish on the left using small crimping edges. Good
climbing all the way.

(30) **Agent Provocateur**   45ft   *E4 6b (PP)* ★★1986
Moving right, almost into the corner. Climb boldly through a
small overhanging bulge (not in the actual corner) until a peg
runner at 15ft is reached, bear left along the break before
moving up. Move back right, small friend, and finish directly
with greater difficulty.

(30a) **Double Trouble**   50ft   *E3 6a (AP)*   1996
A girdle of the wall. Climb *West Point* to the obvious ledge
(insitu pegs stolen May '97) and hand traverse right along the
horizontal break following the line of Double Agent. Move up
and across into the corner and finish as for *Trouble with Lichen*.

(31) **Trouble With Lichen** 40ft *E3 6a (AP)* ★★1975/1985
Climb the clean cut corner bounding the right side of the wall,
micro-wires at half height, to finish with a superb bridging
move on smooth granite. Reaching the crux has become easier due to a certain type of unwanted attention!

(32) **Corner Route**   40ft   *Severe 4a (PP)*   1970
The more broken corner right of *Trouble With Lichen* is
climbed using a series of mantels, some of which are rather
testing.

(33) **Sweet Surrender** 40ft *F7c (E6 6b/c) (WP)* ★★1995
The obvious, colourful, overhanging prow can be climbed on
its left side, via small edges, until the lip is reached. Move up
to the break, containing a letter box niche. Mantel onto this,
before breaking right for the arete and the finish.

(34) **Tag**   40ft   *F7b (E5 6b) (WP)*   ★★1994
The right-hand side of the prow, can be climbed directly up
the steep overhanging face, turning the tip of the arete on its
right to finish. It can be finished out right up the crack but this
only warrants *F7a+ (E4 6b)*.

WESTERN OUTCROP (CENTRAL BAY)

This bay also has the advantage of being in direct alignment to the morning sun, which seems to give the rock a clean, white and warm appearance.

THE CLIMBS

The climbs are described from left to right.

(35) **Mike's Route**   40ft   *Severe 4a (AP)*   1966
Start on the low ridge on the left of the central wall and climb to a large ledge, finish to the left.

(36) **Nocturne**   50ft *Hard Very Severe 5a (AP)* *1986
Climb via a layback flake to the ledge on *Mike's Route*. Continue directly up the obvious small fault above (peg runner). Great finish on good holds.

(37) **Central Route** 60ft *Very Severe 4c (PP)* **1971
Start as for *Nocturne* to the large ledge and then bear right up the obvious fault line to the top. An easier start can be made from the blocks on the left. Bold.

(38) **Second Class Return**   55ft   *E2 5b/c (PP)*   1976
Climb the central slanting groove via difficult moves to a good ledge. Continue up past a peg to join *Central Route* at the top (A serious undertaking).

(39) **One Way Ticket**   60ft   *E2 5b (PP)*   1973
This route takes the left side of the steep smooth slab, right of the groove of *Second Class Return* move left at 30ft onto the ledge, peg insitu, finish as for Second Class Return.

(40) **Chance**   60ft   *E4 5c (NP)*   1988
A bold climb. A difficult mantel on to the right side of the slab, then move left and up (the precise line and grade are unclear). Difficult moves at two thirds height.

(41) **Direct Route** 60ft   *Very Severe 4a (NP)* *1964
The arete on the right of the central bay is climbed to the top.

(42) Back Breaker   50ft   *Very Difficult 4a (PP)*   1969
Zig zag your way up the back corner to finish up the stepped corner more directly.

(43) Sentry Box   40ft   *Severe 4b (WP)*   1974
Right of the corner is an obvious buttress which gives the cheerful line of this route, which has a good finish along large sized cracks.

THE WESTERN OUTCROP

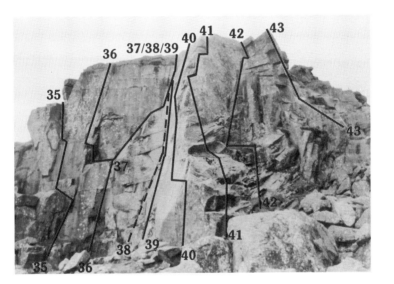

MAIN FACE (LEFT-SIDE)

Andy Grieve on Tag (F7b) Cheesewring Quarry. *Photo: Sean Hawken*

Sean Hawken & Nick Hancock on Le Tour (F7a+) Cheesewring Quarry. *Photo: Andy Grieve*

THE MAIN FACE

On the left of the Main Face is an obvious boulder slope, which provides an easy way down from the top. Descending the slope the first feature on the left is a small bay with a shallow corner, formed by a short wall and a very smooth slab. Next, two short corners are passed, the first provides a mere scramble *The Steps* (Moderate *3a*) while the second is pitch two of *The Purple Revrac* which starts on the boulder slope some 35ft below the corner.

THE CLIMBS

The climbs are described from left to right.

(43a) **Longshank's Leap**   25ft *E1 5c (NP)*   1996

In the bay the shallow corner is climbed curving right to a mantelshelf then directly up to the top. Protected after the mantelshelf but not on the crux. There are two bouldering variations to the lower section. Trending directly up the wall on the left (easier *5b*) or climbing the slab, right, to the crux (harder *6a*).

(43b) **Steps Arete**   40ft   *Severe 4a (AP)*   1996

This little arete between the easy corner of *The Steps* and *The Purple Revrac* provides a bold lead to push into the severe grade with. Climb up into the easy corner then traverse right onto the arete and climb it to the top.

(44) **Purple Revrac**   75ft *Hard Severe 4b (WP)* ★★1969

1: 35ft 4b. Belay at the foot of a square cut boulder half way down the scree slope. Then climb to the base of the corner, via a bore hole and shallow groove. Good moves that are too easy to escape!
2: 40ft 4b. Climb the very popular corner.

(44a) **Heart of Darkness**   85ft   *E2 5b (AP)* 1996

1: 60ft 5b. Start as for *The Purple Revrac* but climb the steep crackline and pillar on the right to pass a hard move; continue up over mantelshelves then move up right, into the corner and peg belay of *Blackberry Wall*.
2: 25ft 5a. The wall on the left is climbed to the top, trending left towards the arete with a tied-off peg for protection.

(45) **Blackberry Wall**   100ft *Hard Very Severe 5b (PP)* 1989
1: 80ft 5b.The large, damp, corner at the bottom of the boulder slope is climbed via a series of mantelshelves to a peg belay (or runner) just below the top.
2: 20ft. Finish up the corner.

(46) **Bird Line**   145ft   *E2 5c (PP)* 1969/1985
1: 120ft 4c. Start by climbing the large rake running right to left into the corner and then head back right over ledges to a belay of large blocks and a bird's nest.
2: 25ft 5c. The next pitch is the groove on the right of the overhang. A good pitch.

(46a) **'Our Carver'**   100ft   *F7c (E5 6b/c) (WP)*   ★1996
Start on the left side of the smooth, striped, overhanging wall below an obvious ramp (this is traversed by the next route *Rampage*).
1: 60ft 6b/c. Climb straight to the start of the ramp and continue up and left through the overhanging striped wall, via a thin fault line (crux), to a large ledge. Move left and up to a belay.
2: 40ft 6a. Follow the curving overlap to the overhang above. Move directly through it and climb straight to the top.

(47) **Rampage**   100ft   *F7b (E5 6b) (WP)*   ★★★1993
Brilliant climbing! Start as for *'Our Carver'*.
1: 75ft 6b. Climb straight up to the sloping ledge and bolt runner. The ramp to the right is followed strenuously to a standing position at its end. Now move up and left (crux) into a steep groove (bolt) which is followed to a peg and friend belay.
2: 25ft 6a. Exposed and exhilarating. The finish takes the obvious challenge directly through the overhang (bolt) at its widest point.

(48) **Hot Lava**   115ft   *F7c (E6 6c) (WP)*   ★★1995
1: 80ft 6c. The overhanging groove down and right of Rampage, is reached via an undercling. Move on up to the top of the ramp, before stepping right and climbing the crack and ledges to peg belay.
2: 35ft 6b. From the belay ledge climb up the corner and then

make a difficult swing out right onto a very rounded edge. Move up and over the small overlap and finish directly up the face

(49) **Simanon Direct** 110ft *Hard Very Severe 4c (PP)* ★★★1967

Probably the best route at its grade in the quarry, and one of the most popular. Start below the hanging chain (which is not supposed to be used).

1: 30ft 4b. Climb the rake with the chain to its fixing stanchion, beware this is very old and rusty, back it up!

2: 40ft 4c. Mantel up and traverse right to a vee groove (nut placement). Climb the groove and then traverse back left and up precariously to a large ledge belay. A bold pitch.

Alternative 5a: A direct variation, continuing straight up the corner to the second belay, escapes the main challenge of the pitch for the price of some harder moves.

3: 40ft 4b. The best pitch. A break on the right allows you to gain the slab above and a superb hand traverse on the exposed slab gains the top.

(50) **Simian** 80ft *E3 5c (AP)* 1987

Start at the chain on *Simanon Direct*. Climb the alternative route to a small stance, move up and right to meet the difficult and fingery crack which shoots right across the top pitch of *Simanon Direct*.

To the right of the Simanon Direct rake is the rake of The Trampoline which leads diagonally left to the corner and base of the 'Wrinkled' wall.

(51) **Mecca** 110ft *E1 5a (AP)* ★1965/74

A climb that evolved over some years from the first ascent of pitch 2 in 1965 to the improvement of the addition of *The Whit Finish* almost a decade later.

1: 40ft 4c. Start left of the rake of *Trampoline*. Climb the short wall onto the rake and take a straight line to a large ledge below a groove in the centre of 'The Wrinkled Wall', belay.

2: 40ft 5a. Climb the groove past a ledge on the right to belay on the vast ledge below the slab. Bold.

3: 30ft 5a. *The Whit Finish*. Move back right, past the top of the groove, and traverse delicately to gain the nose and the top.

Alternative: An easier but poor finish is to climb the slab to a hand traverse and exit via this on the right.

(52) **The Trampoline** 110ft *Hard Very Severe 4c (PP)* ★1965
A superb summer's day excursion.

1: 50ft 4b. Climb the rake trending up and leftwards to a comfortably large ledge below the wrinkled wall. A good belay can be set up here.

2: 60ft 4c. Now climb the open wrinkled corner which is sustained and unprotected, finish up the vegetated corner above.

(53) **Silva Gray**   120ft   *E4 6a (PP)*   ★1967/1987
1: 20ft 5c. Five feet right of *Trampoline* is a shallow groove, climb this to a large ledge.

2: 50ft 5c. Climb the two bore holes on the left at the back to another ledge, move right into a groove (high peg runner) then mantelshelf onto a ledge on the right. Move up past a peg in a groove to gain the next section of ledges and a thread belay.

3: 50ft 6a. Climb the slab to a small groove above and to the right of the overhang, peg. Move diagonally leftwards above the roof to reach two more pegs, swing up onto the slab and finish direct.

(54) **Black Sabbath** 120ft   *E5 6a & A2+ (PP)*   1970/89
Originally a bold artificial climb currently falling uncomfortably between several styles of climbing as the final wall still waits to be freed.

1: 20ft 5c. As for pitch one of *Silva Gray* to the ledge.

2: 40ft 6a. A few feet right of the bore holes of *Silva Gray* an obvious arched groove forms the left hand side of a great slab. This is now shared with *Bored of the Wrings (E5 6a)* which takes the groove complete. Climb the groove to a rusty old bolt head. Gain the small ledge on the left then move up a few feet to a stance in a small niche at the foot of a groove.

3: 60ft A2+. Climb the groove to gain the traverse line of *Gather Darkness* then move right until below the overhanging yellow wall. Yes, it's that old system of aid. Peg your way up the lower of the two diagonal cracks to the top.

NB: New bolts can now be found in this upper section. This is due to it being attempted as a free climb which as yet remains a project.

Right of the groove is a fourteen foot high wall (Gila's Wall).

(55) **Bored of the Wrings**   120ft   *E5 6a (AP)* ★★1989

This gem has sadly seen few ascents, but is judged to be one of the best traditional routes in the quarry
1: 20ft 5c. Either the groove of *Silva Gray* or the wall to the belay of *Silva Gray*.
2. 100ft 6a. Climb the obvious arching groove in its entirety and continue up the top pitch of *Eyefull Tower*.

Boulder up to the large ledge above Gila's Wall where the next climb takes the smooth slab right of Bored of the Wrings.

(56) **Le Tour**   120ft   *F7a+ (E4 6b) (WP)*   ★★1995

1: 90ft 6b. Start slightly to the right of the centre, under the bolt. Move up and then left along a thin horizontal crack line past a friend placement. Move up to another bolt and the roof. Now pull over the overhanging lip (bolt) and move up and right to the iron rod on the stance of *Eyefull Tower*.
2: 30ft 6a. Finish as for *Eyefull Tower*.

(57) **Dead Exit**   120ft   *E4 6a (NP)* ★1986

A bold variation on *High Noon*. Start on the left of *Gila's Wall*.
1: 95ft 6a. Go straight up over the overhang via a difficult mantelshelf and continue direct to the first iron spike on *Eyefull Tower*, move right and ascend the right side of the large slab with ground fall potential to a junction with *High Noon* and it's belay.
2: 25ft 5c. Above is an overhang, make stretchy moves to finish direct.

The floor below the short wall here, *Gila's Wall*, has been filled by a couple of industrious local climbers. Thanks to their hard efforts we can now enjoy the bouldering, without having to pay dearly for failing to complete the move. To the right of *Gila's Wall (5b)*, the first and easiest climb on the right of this wall, there is a chimney; *Merlin's Chimney (4b)*, this gives the start of one of the most popular climbs in the quarry.

(58) **Eyefull Tower** 120ft *E2 6a (AP)* ★★★1967/86

Don't miss out on this classic because you're not up to the 6a moves! It's great climbed in its original style which uses the insitu protection for aid (5a).

1: 55ft 5a. Climb *Merlin's Chimney* to a ledge. Surmount *The Wizard's Hat* (the triangular block above) and from its summit move left to a ledge in the bottom of a groove (iron spike runner). Continue to a ledge and further iron spike, belay.

2: 65ft 6a. Move up and through the overlap above (peg runners) to a square cut ledge with two old bolts. Now climb the groove (crux) by laybacking the crack (using the insitu gear for aid here, reduces the pitch to 5a) to gain the mantelshelf (thread runner). Easier moves lead to the top.

> An easy access from the left-hand side of the *Central Bay*, below the great prow of the *Central Overhang* to the ledges of the main wall is via *Merlin's Traverse* 35ft Difficult. From just above the start of the *High Noon* traverse easily around the base of *The Wizard's Hat* until the ledges above *Gila's Wall* are reached.

(59) **High Noon** 120ft *E3 5c (PP)* ★★1967/1986

A bold and intimidating lead.

1: 35ft 5a. The right-hand crack at the back of the Wizard's Hat to belay on top.

2: 60ft 5b. Move up and then diagonally right on large ledges into the Central Bay and up to an old bolt. Move right to gain the mantelshelf above the bolt and up to a small overlap on the arete. Move left to a ledge and bolt belay.

3: 25ft 5c. Above the belay is an overhang. Make a long reach to good holds and finish direct past one peg runner.

> *The next route is a quality climb in a superb position. Although written as two pitches it makes a great climb when completed in one pitch.*

(60) **Mauritius** 120ft *E5 6b/c (F7b) (AP)* ★★★1989

1: 90ft 6b/c. Start in the Central Bay, below the main overhanging headwall at a sharp rib. Climb diagonally leftwards past a peg runner to the bolt on pitch one of *High Noon*. Step right and boldly climb the groove to a steep wall above past

bolt runners to the belay of *High Noon*.
2: 30ft 6a. Continue on up right onto the spectacular hanging slab, following this to its end and then finish direct.

(60a) **Black Panther**   120ft   *C5 6b & A3 (AP)*   1970/93

Len Benstead's artificial climbing *Tour de Force* has partially been superseded by *Real Live Wire*. Nevertheless *Black Panther* is the only climb to 'top out' in the area right of the Central Overhang.
1: 50ft 5a. As for *High Noon* to belay at the bolt on pitch two.
2: 40ft 6b. Continue up into the corner to join the black ramp (now climbed free) of *Real Live Wire* and continue up this to a projecting ledge and belay.
3: 30ft A3. From here peg up the vertical crack behind to the top using an assortment of pitons.

(60b) **Super Indirect**   145ft *E4 6a & A2 (AP)*   1970

A fine artificial traverse of the Central Bay which still has to see a completely free ascent. Start on a large platform in the middle of the Central Bay, left of an old iron ring.
1: 45ft 6a. Climb the left side of the detached pedestal, left around the nose and up and left to join *High Noon* at the bolt on pitch 2. To this point the climb, more or less, shares the line of *Mauritius* so banging in pegs here will now be resented! Continue up a small slab and take a peg belay on the ledge above.
2: 55ft A2. Move right and step down to place a blade peg in the horizontal crack which continues around beneath the overhang. Traverse right entirely on aid (blades, insitu bolts and skyhooks) to pull around into the gully of *Scapegoat*.
3: 45ft. As *Scapegoat* to exit (V.Diff)

(61) **Real Live Wire**   80ft   *F7b (E5 6b) (WP)* ★★1993

The climb starts up a smooth shallow groove in the middle of the Central Bay and is defined by a line of bolts on the left. Climb the groove in its entirety to pull precariously onto the rounded ledge. Move leftwards up to the black ramp and climb this to a lower off at its end.

Note: It is best to attempt to lower off on at least 2 bolts.

(62) **Psychokiller**   *80ft   E6 6c (F7c+) (PP)*★★★1988
A strenuous challenge using the old bolt ladder in the Central
Bay for protection. Start left of the ladder. Climb to a poor bolt
and pass this to a resting place below the niche (friend 2),
move up into the niche and exit through its roof. Continue to
the bolt lower-off.
Note: It is best to lower off on at least two bolts.

(63) **Wring the Changes**   80ft   *E6 6c (F7c) (AP)* ★1988
To the right of *Psychokiller* is the so called 'Drainpipe', start
here for another exacting test. Climb following various bolts
and a peg past a hanging slab on the right to bear left to the bolt
lower off.
Note : It is best to attempt to lower off on at least 2 bolts.

(64) **Spectral Radius**   *75ft A2/3 (AP)*   1970
A high traverse just below the Central Overhang and another
old aid line, which has yet to see a free ascent. Start at the last
stance of *High Noon*.
Using a peg high on the right-hand side of the ledge, swing
down and right and under the Central Overhang. Continue on
the same line to reach a ledge with a bolt at its far end. Place a
peg as far right as possible. Rope down 20ft to the old bolts on
Super Indirect and finish as for this climb.

THE FORTRESS
AND FORTRESS WALL

The steep wall, right of the *Central Bay* has a large recess
above it. This is *The Fortress*. The wall below contains climbs in
the mid–E grades. The first of these takes the prominent arete
on the left of the wall dividing it from the *Central Bay*.

(65) **Rene**   120ft   *E4 6a (PP)*   1975/91
1: 80ft 6a. Climb to a ledge (high bolt) and pull over the small
overhang to gain a groove and second bolt runner. Continue
to a large ledge and thread belay. Bold.
2: 40ft 4a. The *Scapegoat* gully above is taken to the top.

(66) **Warrior**   120ft   *F6c+ (E3 5c) (WP)* ★★★1970/88
1: 80ft 5c. An open bore hole leads to the steep groove line
10ft right of *Rene*. Climb this passing various pegs and new

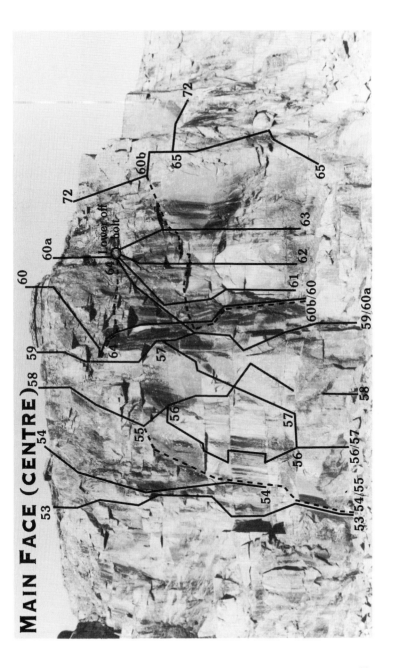

MAIN FACE (CENTRE)

89

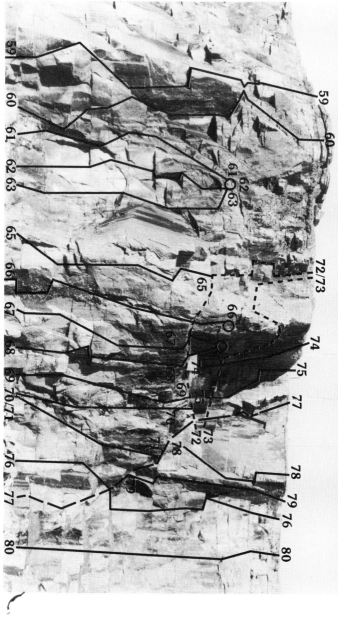

MAIN FACE (CENTRE) FORTRESS & FORTRESS WALL

bolts to a peg on the large ledge above on the left, before moving up to clip into the peg/bolt lower-off.

2. 40ft. Finish up any of the Fortress routes; *Khyber Wall* is recommended.

(67) **Friend or Foe?**   110ft   *F7a+ (E4 6b) (WP)* ★1991

Start almost at the same point as *Warrior* but instead of climbing to the borehole, trend right and move on up the wall.

1: 80ft 6b. Climb the small ramped groove to continue up the fault through the crux to the mantel, this will enable you to gain the ledge on the right. Finish directly up the wall to the Fortress. Peg belay.

2: 30ft 4a. Continue up the left wall of the Fortress or descend from the *Warrior* lower-off.

(68) **Sling Shot**   80ft   *F7b (E5 6b) (WP)*   1995

Six feet right of *Friend or Foe?* A protruding rib marks the start of this route. Climb the rib to the top and then move on up the short overhanging bulge, using a powerful undercut. Finish directly up the steep wall to a lower-off.

(69) **Special Offer**   110ft   *E3 6a (AP)*   1967/88

A more direct and free variation of the 1960's aid climb *Expensive A2*. Start beneath a peg in the centre of the wall.

1: 80ft 6a. Climb up to and past a peg (crux), continue up a groove (peg) and climb up the wall past another peg to reach the fortress.

2: 30ft. As for Friend or Foe?

(70) **Bump Start**   80ft   *E3 5c (PP)*   1988

Climb the bore hole and shallow groove right of *Special Offer* directly to the top.

(71) **Children in Need**   100ft *E3 5b (PP)* 1988

Start as for *Bump Start* and climb, trending right, up the weakness past an insitu peg. Finish to the far right, and then climb the back of the Fortress.

The next four climbs all start up in the Fortress. They can be approached either by abseil or better still by climbing the first two pitches of Traitor's Gate (Hard Severe) for which they can be considered alternative finishes.

(72) **Scapegoat**   85ft *Very Difficult 4a (PP)* ★1965

The lower traverse out of The Fortress starts from the pitch 2
belay of *Traitor's Gate*.
1: 40ft 4a. Traverse the narrowing base ledge of The Fortress
left, past a block and around an awkward corner. Here the
ledge narrows towards the end giving truly sensational
exposure (protection, not available to the pioneers, can be
found utilising the peg in *Friend or Foe?*) Belay at a bore hole
on the far side of the gully.
2: 45ft 3c. Easily up the gully to the top.

(73) **Pinnacle Route**   75ft *Very Difficult 4b (PP)* ★1965

The higher traverse out of The Fortress with dramatic aspects
and a very traditional feel.
1: 40ft 4b. Climb left along the upper ledge to the pinnacle,
which makes a very exposed seat, (and pray the block stays!).
Then move out left into the gully to belay.
2: 35ft 3c. Take the easiest line out.

(74) **Fortress Indirect**   30ft   *Severe 4a (PP)*   1965

The left wall of the Fortress above the pinnacle has obvious
holds on it. Very exposed.

(75) **Fortress Direct**   35ft   *Very Difficult 4a (PP)*   1965

Take the true (left hand) corner at the back of The Fortress.

The following climbs start below The Fortress.

(76) **Anthony**   90ft   *Hard Very Severe 4c (NP)*   1965

This route has very vegetated ledges and starts up the series of
mantels left of the black slab with the deep crack in it.
1: 30ft 4b. Climb the mantels to the large ledge with the iron
ring belay.
2: 60ft 4c. Climb the left edge of the orange slab until it is
possible to move left into the corner and finish via more mantels.

(77) **Traitor's Gate**   90ft   *Hard Severe 4b (PP)* ★1965

The easiest way up into The Fortress giving good climbing
when dry but after any rain the crux seeps heavily. The crux
protection on pitch 2 is one of the oldest and worst placed
pegs (behind a very hollow flake) in the quarry. Do not expect

it to stay in if you load it.

1: 30ft 4a. Climb the deep crack splitting a small black slab below and right of The Fortress to a large ledge. An old iron ring, hidden in grass, provides a belay.

2: 30ft 4b. Traverse left and up past the dangerous old peg, into The Fortress and up to a good thread belay.

3: 30ft 4a. Climb the right-hand stepped corner in the back of The Fortress.

The prominent sharp right hand arete of The Fortress produces superbly positioned climbing. Abseil in or as described below, approach via Traitor's Gate.

(78) **Khyber Wall**   80ft *E2 5c (WP)* ★★★1970/1986

1: 50ft 4b. As for *Traitor's Gate* into The Fortress (belay next to the arete on a large block).

2: 30ft 5c. Climb the left-hand side of the arete to the over-hang. Turn this on its left to gain a vertical break and the finish.

(79) **Khyber Pass**   80ft *E4 6a (AP)* ★1993

Takes the arete on its right side. It has three bolts, but is still a bold lead.

1: 30ft 4a. Climb *Traitor's Gate* to a large ledge and the iron ring.

2 50ft 6a. Climb as if starting pitch 2 of *Traitor's Gate* but move right onto a sloped ramp and then directly up to the base of the arete (bolt). Continue up the right-hand side of the arete past two bolts, staying with the arete until the overhang is reached. Break right and climb the thin crack (nut protection) to the crux and the top.

ORANGE SLAB
AND LEMON TREE AREA

Right of *Anthony* there is a distinct orange slab. Which can easily be gained by climbing up to a large grassy ledge, via a couple of mantels.

(80) **Young Hunting**   90ft *E3 5c (PP)*   1972/86

Climb the left edge of the orange slab to the top, turn the overhang on the left and exit to ledges.

(81) **Sarah Louise**   80ft   *E2/3 5b (PP)*   1986

Climb the centre of the orange slab and then climb on through the overhanging bulge as directly as possible (bold).

(82) **Juliet's Balcony** 90ft *Hard Very Severe 5a (AP)* ★1967
Provides a very enjoyable tour up the right hand side of the orange slab.
1: 30ft 4b. Contrived but pleasant. From below a boulder on the ledge at the base of the orange slab climb directly to it avoiding the easy break on the right.
2: 60ft 5a. Take a line of good holds starting 10ft left of the right-hand edge of the slab and climb diagonally right to the top of the slab and peg runners. Gain the balcony on the right by an awkward move (5a), or alternatively finish directly above the pegs at (5b).

Right of the orange slab the overhanging wall offers the
following climbs. Belay on the large ledge below
the bulging wall.

(83) **Beast of Revelation** 90ft *E1 4c (PP)* 1969
1: 30ft. Climb up the easy break right of *Juliet's Balcony* to a huge grassy ledge, nut belay on the right. The overhanging wall above has a diagonal fault running left.
2: 60ft 4c. Up the fault on a series of flakes. A bold route.

(84) **The Crystal Maze** 60ft *E3 5c (AP)* 1995
Belay as for pitch 1 of *Beast of Revelation* on the grassy ledge. Climb directly up the black slab to the foot of the overhanging face. Follow a line up the left side of the face. Climb through two patches of crystals. In situ pegs have been removed.

(85) **Gone to Pot** 60ft *E3 6a (F6c+) (WP)* 1993
This pitch provides fingery climbing directly up the right-hand side of the overhanging wall, peg runners (removed). Start from the grassy ledge of *Beast of Revelation*.
Follow the first 20ft of *Crystal Maze* before moving right and climbing the blankest section of the wall.

(86) **Man of Double Deed** 85ft *Hard Severe 4b (WP)* 1969
Pleasant climbing and a good finish which helps make up for its rather escapable nature.
1: 30ft. Climb easily to the grass ledge.
2: 55ft 4b. Climb the right edge of the steep wall avoiding the corner on the right (88–*Unnamed*) to a good thread runner

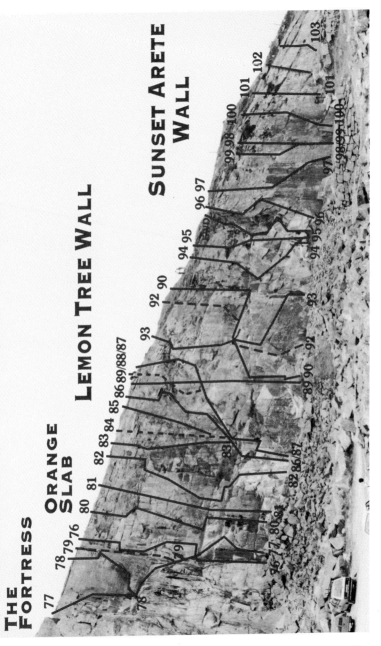

THE
FORTRESS

ORANGE
SLAB

LEMON TREE WALL

SUNSET ARETE
WALL

95

Nick Hancock on Rampage (F7b) Cheesewring Quarry. *Photo: Sean Hawken*

below a small overhang which is turned on the left on excellent holds.

Right of the overhanging wall the following climbs are extremely popular. It is also possible to link pitches and variations of these routes to create interesting combinations. Let your imagination run riot but remember you are unlikely to discover anything that is actually new.

(87) **Lemon Tree**   90ft *Hard Severe 4b (AP)*   ★★1965

1: 45ft 4a. Start on the right side of the easy break, climb stepped ledges to a short steep wall and peg belay. Back it up!
2: 45ft 4b. Move up and right (crux). Climb to a hollow above the wall (thread runner) and move left, past the curious hollow, to the top.

(88) **Unnamed**   45ft   *Severe 4b (AP)*   1966

A variation on *Lemon Tree* which gives some excellent climbing. From the belay of pitch 1 of *Lemon Tree* move left to a square cut corner and climb this, passing a curious pocket, to join the last few moves of *Lemon Tree*.

(89) **The Vandal**   85ft   *E3 6a (AP)*   1968/86

Start on the flat wall just left of *Peter*.
1: 45ft 6a. Follow the thin crack and climb to a ledge then up the flat wall above via a crack.
2: 40ft 6a. Tackle the overhanging shield wall directly above the peg of *Lemon Tree*.

(90) **Peter**   75ft   *Very Difficult 4a (AP)*   ★1964

The first climb recorded in the quarry. Start at the obvious break right of the smooth wall of *The Vandal* where a short ramp leads to a shallow corner.
1: 35ft 4a. Up the ramp then climb the corner to belay around the projecting block/ledge.
2: 40ft 3c. Walk right, down the ledge and climb the easy break to its end to another ledge just short of the top. Contrived but pleasing, take an ascending line of holds back left to finish, ignoring the obvious exit.

(91) **Figuzzi**   80ft   *Hard Severe* 4b (AP) ★★1970s

A mix of obvious good pitches from other climbs producing some of the best Hard Severe climbing on this part of the cliff.
1: 50ft 4b. Climb the start of *Peter* to the left side of the large ledge, move up and diagonally left to the *Lemon Tree* belay.
2: 30ft 4b. Climb the corner of *Unnamed* to the thread runner, now finish left under the overhang as for *Man of Double Deed*.

(92) **Star Fox**   65ft *Hard Very Severe* 5a (PP) ★1969

Popular and bold with both pitches being a bit like boulder problems!
1: 30ft 5a. Five feet right of *Peter* is a curved groove containing a borehole scar, climb here using the curved groove to move up to the large ledge and belay.
2: 35ft 4c. Move down the ledge and surmount the bulging wall on spaced holds some of which may be loose at the start.

The flat black wall to the right has a thin horizontal ledge at half height which runs fully across the length of the wall. There are a selection of hard boulder problems here, which finish at this thin ledge. For details see the bouldering guide at the end of the section.

(93) **Thorndyke**   90ft   *Very Severe* 4c (PP)   1965

Start on the right of the black wall.
1: 40ft 4c. At the right hand side of the black wall the ledge comes to within 8ft of the ground, gain this and then traverse left to the ledge of *Peter*.
2: 50ft 4c. Climb left and then back right on the left edge of the bulging wall. Finish easily above.

(94) **Jane**   60ft   *Difficult 4a (PP)*   1965

Midway between the large gully which constitutes the Easy Way Down and *Thorndyke* is a prominent ledge. Start left of the EWD and move up to the ledge where a tricky mantelshelf leads to easier climbing and the top.

Often climbed but never published. I have purposely included the following climb to aid beginners in finding a suitable training area.

(95) **Sue**   60ft   *Moderate 3b (PP)*   1960s

Start about six feet right of *Jane*. Climb the large ledges to gain the back corner. Now climb directly to the top.

Editor's Note: It seems you can't keep a useful scramble down! When three climbers from RAF Brampton dared to write *Sue* up as a new climb in the Cheesewring Hut Log Book (29 August 1974) it prompted a terse comment. This was because it was then considered part of the Easy Way Down! The re-working of the early 1980s opened up the eastern side of the quarry and reduced the need of this EWD which has resulted in the gully becoming popular for instructing beginners.

The right hand buttress of the Main Wall, right of the Easy Way Down, is a steep slab, with a distinctive rust and black colouring. The rock is geologically different here and feels very different to the rest of the quarry.

(96) **Sunset Arete**   40ft   *Very Severe 4b (AP)*   1972

The undercut arete on the right of the EWD is gained by an ascending traverse from the left following the broken groove.

(97) **Total Recall**   40ft   *E1 5a (AP)*   1995

Start at the beginning of the right to left diagonal break. Climb up this almost to its end. Then shoot straight up the blank looking wall above.

(98) **Cheese Disease**   35ft   *E1 5a (NP)*   1989

Start 20ft right of the arete where a ledge stands 5ft off the ground. Starting just left of this ledge climb directly to the top finishing left of a perched block.

(99) **P.M.C.**   35ft   *E1 5a (NP)*   1991

At approximately half height. A variation to the previous route runs more to the left again. It sadly no longer supports its protection and seems to have lost some holds.

(100) **Risky**   35ft   *Very Severe 4b (PP)*   1968

Start on the ledge and climb directly past a difficult move at half height and then move right to finish. Requires RP's, micro nuts or a steady leader!

(101) **Wall Flower**   20ft   *Hard Severe 4b (PP)*   1989

Right of *Risky* there is a depression in the rock. Climb out of the depression and bear left towards the finish of *Risky*.

(102) **Forty Five**   20ft   *Very Difficult 4c (NP)*   1968
Start 6ft right of *Risky* at a stepped corner. A single difficult move gains the start and the rest of the climbing is disproportionately easy but still pleasant.

(103) **Sarah**   25ft   *Very Difficult 4a (AP)*   1960s
Right again approximately 10ft, there is a small fold that can be climbed. Finish via cracks moving left to the top.

THE TRAVERSES

Cheesewring Quarry, with its hard and demanding left-hand Main Wall, Central Overhangs and easier right-hand side, sadly does not lend itself to a continuous girdle traverse of a sustained or similar standard. Four separate traverses have, therefore, resulted: *Gather Darkness, Spectral Radius* (already described) and *Combine* which could be linked via *Scapegoat* (already described).

(104) **Gather Darkness**   330ft   *E3 5c (AP)*   ★★1970
A fine expedition across the Main Wall. Start as for *The Purple Revrac*.
1: 125ft 4c. Climb pitch one of *The Purple Revrac* until it is possible to break right and make an ascending traverse right to the final belay of *Simanon Direct*.
2: 60ft 4c. Down-climb *Simanon Direct* to below the vee groove and move right to belay below the wrinkled wall of *Mecca*
3: 40ft 4c. Follow *Mecca* until a traverse right leads to the stance of *Silva Gray*.
4: 80ft 5c. A rising traverse right is awkward but gets you to the bolts on pitch two of *Eyefull Tower*, move right to the last stance of *High Noon*.
5: Finishes. The traditional, and original, finish is to abseil off. Alternatives are to finish as for *High Noon* (25ft, 5c) or to join *Spectral Radius* and continue traversing.

(105) **Combine**   200ft   *Difficult 4a (AP)*   1965
A useful climb for beginners, easy and unintimidating it allows familiarisation with the unique nature of quarry climbing.
1: 30ft 4a.   As for *Traitor's Gate* then right to the belay of *Juliet's Balcony*.

2: 110ft 3a. Easily right on vast ledges to the first belay on Peter.
3: 60ft 4a. Follow Peter to the top or traverse on to finish up *Jane* or *Sue*.

CHEESEWRING BOULDERING

ON THE TOP

Above the quarry is **The Cheesewring** after which the quarry is named, this is a natural formation of horizontally arranged rounded blocks with the top most one being the largest. This sports two extended boulder problems, the superb *Northside Route* 18ft *(5c)* takes the overhangs on the north side! Which is the side farthest from the quarry. To the left (top side) is the rounded arete of the *North-easterly Route* which can be ascended at (6a).

One short route exists. *Nomadic Jam Session* 25ft *E2 5c* climbs the pinned boulders on the quarry side to a large roof, step left around the corner and move directly to the top. Another true gritstone style boulder problem can be found on the furthest 'Cheesewring type' formations at the top of the hill by climbing the very prominent nose on the lower side overhang (6b).

IN THE QUARRY

Moving anti-clockwise starting at the entrance of the quarry, the **Southern Outcrop** holds a right to left, low level, full length traverse at (6b).The flat wall right of *Star Fox* has several problems, (left to right) beginning with the *Star Fox* start at (5a), move over 4ft directly under the arch (6a) followed by a second problem up the groove at (6b). In the centre of the slab is a problematic (6a), there then follows a very fingery test climbing up the blankest section of the wall using the extremely thin horizontal break at (6c), the final problem on the flat wall almost in the corner is (5a). These challenges finish at the larger horizontal break used by *Thorndyke*.

Moving over into the **Central Bay** you can find a small right-hand arete with a sloping grassy base; climb this still at (6a) despite some recent chipping! In the *Merlin's Chimney* area is the flat wall *Gila's Wall* which is also the name of the problem just left of the chimney. Moving left to right along the wall; firstly the groove of *Silva Gray* can be beaten at (5c), the bulge of the wall is (6b) then the start of *Dead Exit* gives a (6a) mantel, right of this the wall can be climbed using a selection of different holds at (5a/b). The original line of *Gila's Wall* contained a band of amethyst and consequently geologists (not withstanding the possibility of the odd unscrupulous climber) have vandalised it badly, reducing the technical standard considerably. *Merlin's Chimney* itself is (4b), whilst the outside hanging arete is a stretchy (6a) and the groove just to the right is (6b). The large groove right still awaits an ascent but has been climbed up to half height, then traversed right along a thin break (6a).

At the top of the boulder slope the bay of *Longshank's Leap* (5c) offers the bouldering variations as already described.

Almost back at the entrance (left to right) the start of *Dwarf's Dream*, the inside corner is (5c), the arete can be ascended at (5c) and finally the cracked face, moving right to finish is (5b).

Caroline Carpenter on Purple Revrac (HS 4b) Cheesewring.   *Photo: Sean Hawken*

GOLD DIGGINGS QUARRY

The numbers on the diagram correspond to the numbers of the climbs given in the text.

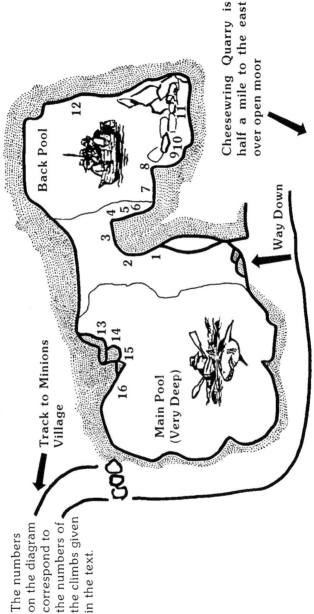

Track to Minions Village

Main Pool (Very Deep)

Back Pool

Way Down

Cheesewring Quarry is half a mile to the east over open moor

GOLD DIGGINGS QUARRY

OS Sheet 201 GR 249724

These flooded workings are half a mile west of the Cheesewring Quarry. They are privately owned and discretion should by used when climbing here. The quarry is often used in the summer by groups picnicking and taking a swim in the deeper first pool.

There is also the challenge of diving off the various platforms that abound the quarry rim. The highest being about 45ft and believe me, it takes some doing. But **be warned, diving into this pool is dangerous,** there are the remains of old cranes just below the surface; like climbing you do it at your own risk!

HOW TO FIND

From Minions village (*see* Cheesewring Quarry approach) it is possible to walk to Gold Diggings Quarry. Park in the Hurlers car park on the south side of the village, then follow the track past the Hurlers and on to Gold Diggings, a walk of about a mile and a half. Alternatively, drive up to Cheesewring Quarry, leave the car and walk west to Gold Diggings which is clearly visible on the next hill. This walk is over open moor so watch out if the weather changes and the mist descends, it's easy to get lost on the way back!

THE CLIMBS

The climbs are described from right to left. Starting with your back to the main pond at the right edge of the rocks that bound the left side of the smallest pool.

(1) **Cue**   18ft   *Difficult 3c (PP)*   circa 1975
On the left of the rocks next to the pool. Surmount the broken short wall via the broken ledges, to gain the top.

(2) **Cue 2**   18ft   *Moderate 3a (AP)*   circa 1975
On the short corner. Climb the harder start to gain the ledges above and take the line of least resistance to the top.

(3) **Barney**   18ft   *Very Difficult 4b (AP)*   circa 1975
Start around the corner in the centre of the short face with the
camp fire burn marks on it. Climb via the small broken vertical
crack, to gain the large ledge above. From here mantelshelf
directly up the remaining face to the top.

*Moving left around the corner, stand with your back to the
second pool, to see the right-hand arete and the steep short
face to your left.*

(4) **McGrew**   20ft   *Hard Severe 4b (PP)*   circa 1975
Climb the right-hand arete directly. The holds just before the
top are a little dubious and should be handled with great respect.

(5) **Cuthbert**   20ft   *Very Severe 4c (PP)*   circa 1975
Move directly up the centre of this short wall, without veering
to the left or the right. Hard moves in the centre on dubious
small holds will leave you concerned about the quality of the
top which, thankfully, is better.

(6) **Dribble**   20ft   *Severe 4b (PP)*   circa 1975
The left hand edge is the most disappointing of these three
routes. Climb up onto a small lip before gaining the top.

*There are two ways of getting to this face. Either you can
walk around to the far side and scrabble down. Or, much
more fun, you can jump over the water in the back corner,
having made the transition over to the jutting rock, that
looks like a face.*

(7) **Grub**   35ft   *Very Severe 4c (AP)*   ★circa 1975
Start below the overhanging nose. Pull up and over this with
difficulty, to gain a ledge. Climb up the detached block, to its
top. Finish directly up the wall above.

(8) **Mirror Mirror**   35ft   *E2 5b (AP)*   ★1986
Start as for *Grub*. Take the face shaped arete on the right and
surmount the overhang then move left to finish directly up the
exposed arete (peg runner).

(9) **Florence**   25ft   *Very Difficult 4a (AP)*   circa 1975
Starts left, around the corner from *Mirror Mirror* in the stepped
back corner which is easily climbed past an old bolt (placed
by, and for the use of an outdoor activity centre). Harder
moves at half height, allow access on up to the top.

(10) **Zebedee**   25ft   *Severe 4b (PP)*   circa 1975
Left of Florence is a small but sharp arete. Climb the arete on
the face that looks out onto the water. Good climbing with
crisp holds.

(11) **Dougal**   25ft   *Severe 4a (PP)*   circa 1975
Starts on the next short wall left with the very flat top. Climb
up the centre of the wall, trending left as height is gained.
Finish on the left side of the flat top.

*The next climb stands alone on the far back wall of the rear
pool. It is advisable to inspect the pegs before attempting
this climb, they are getting very old!*

(12) **Barbecue Wood**   30ft   *E2 5b (AP)*   1986
Climb the crack-line with two peg runners in the wall at the
back of the quarry.

*Moving back into the main pool area now. As you stand
with your back to the 'tiny' little pool, you can see the main
wall opposite. To gain access to this wall it is possible to
traverse and leap in from the right. The following climb
starts on a small platform just above water level.*

(13) **Hamamelis**   45ft   *E2 5c (AP)*   1986
Takes the groove and overhanging headwall at the far end of
the lake. From a ledge climb the groove to a hand traverse
line. Follow this to the left and finish up the steep crack (two
peg runners).

(14) **Dylan**   40ft   *Severe 4c (AP)*   circa 1975
Start on the same platform as *Hamamelis*. Climb directly up
the deep groove to the top. The corner has become covered in
lichen due to a lack of ascents.

(15) **Divers' Route**   40ft   *Severe 4c (PP)*   circa 1975

Used by divers to choose the height from which they wish to jump! Pull up on to the ledge to the left. From here the next move is height dependent, if you are short it is at least a grade harder. Jump and grab the next ledge, mantel up to gain another ledge. The top is then easily reached.

(16) **The Darkness Beckons**   40ft   *F7a+ (E4 6b) (WP)* ★1995

The quarry's test piece. The climb requires an abseil approach allowing the belayer to create a hanging belay at the base of the wall, just above water level. Follow the bolt line and climb directly up the steep wall on small but solid holds. Complex moves at half height.

THE BODMIN MOOR TORS

Landranger, OS Sheets 200 & 201

Here you feel all the charismatic remoteness of Bodmin Moor as you climb or boulder on these beautiful tors. The chance of being disturbed is always slim, especially in the winter. At most you are only likely to see a couple of lost ramblers, or a few moorland ponies and of course the local woolly female talent: 'if ewe know what I mean!' **Warning:** At certain times of the year, the moors are prolific with sheep ticks.

HOW TO FIND

To find these areas, drive towards Launceston from Liskeard on the B3254. On entering the small hamlet of Middlewood, turn left, just before the bridge. Follow this road to its end, where you can park on the right before a farm gate.

On your left, to the South as you walk along the track, is the long Kilmar Tor. Bearah Tor is only visible behind it, once you have hiked up to the top. On the right is Hawk's Tor and ahead on the right is Trewortha Tor.

KILMAR TOR

GR 253749

At 1296ft, the rock-strewn summit ridge of Kilmar, nearly half a mile long, was likened to The Great Wall of China in August 1802 when Thomas Bond and his friend scaled the 'Eastern' and 'Western Turrets.' Long before the modern sport began they gave East Cornwall its claim to having the oldest recorded rock climbs. Although they were hunting for 'druidical basins' and not new routes, Bond certainly discovered the thrill of climbing. Yes, it all started here, folks. At a similar standard to Napes Needle, too!

The Eastern Turret and Western Turret, which is sometimes called The Kilmarth, are the obvious, tallest rock piles at the east and western ends of the ridge. The Western Turret (28ft) is the most dramatic as it appears to balance on the ridge, undercut on both sides. Both turrets can easily be climbed in a variety of ways at Difficult standard. There are two modern climbs you'll need your gear for. The north facing overhanging wall holds the routes.

THE CLIMBS.

The climbs are described left to right.

Special Llama   35ft   *E5 6a (AP)* ★★1990
The moor's best kept secret. Climb the centre of the overhanging face, via the breaks to finish by pulling over on the small flake.

Sleepy Hollow   35ft   *E1 5b (AP)* ★1995
A superb little gem. On the right a small corner containing a vertical crack can be found, step up before moving out right to tackle the wall above on brilliant holds.

Kilmar Tor also has a large amount of rarely used bouldering. There is enough to keep even the most avid bouldering fanatic content.

BEARAH TOR

GR 253749

Within view of Kilmar Tor across what appears to be an African safari plain is another interesting and beautiful Tor, Bearah Tor. There is a small amount of explored but unrecorded bouldering here and even the potential for a couple of short climbs. There is a small private quarry on the tor which may be in use from time to time.

TREWORTHA TOR

GR 244757

Furthest away from the comforts of the car, Trewortha, should not be ignored. It has plenty of bouldering, there is a short chimney which R. G. Folkard noted in 1941 and one excellent climb. You will find this hidden treasure on the right as you walk over to the Tor. The wall containing the route is lower than the level you walk in at, so you're likely to see the top first.

THE CLIMB

Just Good Friends   35ft   *VS 5a (WP)* ★★1995
A little delight. Climb directly up the centre of the wall on a
series of flakes. Finish slightly right via another flake.

*The bouldering remains unrecorded for those with the enter-
prise to rediscover.*

HAWK'S TOR

From the road Hawk's Tor, at 1079ft, looks really impressive.
Sadly, only 25ft high, it is somewhat shorter than it at first
appears. However, if you like short, solid, problematic granite
climbing this is the place for you. There are climbs of all
grades, the easier ones were recorded by R. G. Folkard in
1941. During the '60s and '70s the Minions Group scrambled
all over the place and never bothered to write up a thing believing it should be left for fun days and picnics! There are
numerous boulder problems, so seek out this quiet venue for
some solid fun but beware! There have been several sightings
of a black puma here. **Warning:** all wimps should carry tape
for their soft handy pandies, and note: The Beast is out there
somewhere!

Because so much is obvious, short, safe and easy to solo up to
Severe and even Very Severe the older climbs have been left
out of earlier guides. This has drawn criticism in the past, notably from the late Peter Biven in his review of the 1973 guide.
For continuity and the benefit of future guides we have included them here as the crag is now becoming developed.

THE CLIMBS

*The climbs are described from left (west) to right (east) as
you look at the South Face of the Tor which is a long narrow
granite ridge running West to East. There is a prominent
break about two thirds of the way along from its western end
which divides the long, low part of the ridge from The Cat's*

Head Rock, the highest part of the tor. The western end of South Face is marked by a pinnacle separated from the ridge by a deep chimney immediately right of which is the unmistakable 8ft horizontal roof of TDK. The grades here are comparatively stiff, this is due to the climbs being short.

(1) **Pinnacle Chimney**   27ft   *Difficult 3c (AP)*   1941

At the end of the South Face, climb the short slab to gain the chimney and finish on the pinnacle.

(2) **West Chimney**   34ft   *Very Difficult 4a (AP)*   1941

A variation on the chimney which is climbed in its entirety before finishing by a bold move up onto the top of the main ridge.

(3) **TDK**   34ft   *E3 6b (WP)*   ★1986

A true grit style problem. Of the two cracks in the 8ft horizontal overhang, climb the left-hand one, then mantel over the lip to finish.

Note: the right-hand crack in the overhang was used in the '60s to practise the old style of aid climbing, but using nuts rather than pitons, so as not to damage the rock. Protected by top rope because the nuts pulled once the climber had passed them, this might still be a good game for those who want to try 'the old ways!' Camming devices should now make leading it a doddle.

(4) **The Recollection**   28ft   *Hard Severe 4b (WP)*   1960s

An old favourite. Climb up into the corner formed by the right-hand side of the *TDK* overhang and the face where pleasant bridging provides good moves to the top.

15ft right of TDK a protruding block, The Roman Nose, juts out to form another smaller overhang. On its left is:

(5) **Crack 'n' Up**   23ft   *Very Difficult 4b (AP)*   1960s

Climb the face via the crack on the left of *The Roman Nose* then directly up the face above.

(6) **The Roman Nose**   23ft   *Difficult 4a (AP)*   1941

Start 12ft right of *Crack 'n' Up* by stepping up onto a low ledge and traversing back left to climb the corner formed by the right side of the nose and the face, then up the wall above.

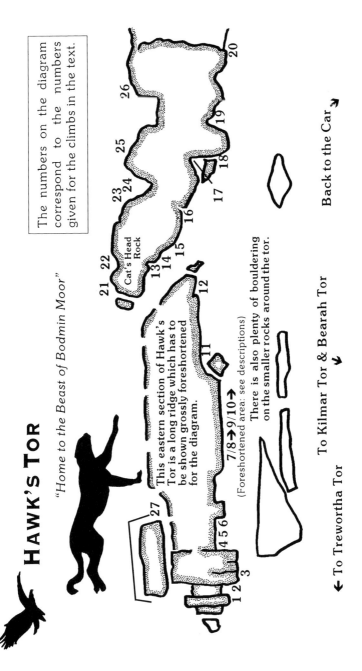

HAWK'S TOR

"Home to the Beast of Bodmin Moor"

The numbers on the diagram correspond to the numbers given for the climbs in the text.

26

20

19

25

23 24

18

17

16

21 22

Cat's Head Rock

15

14

13

12

11

This eastern section of Hawk's Tor is a long ridge which has to be shown grossly foreshortened for the diagram.

(Foreshortened area: see descriptions)

7/8→9/10→

There is also plenty of bouldering on the smaller rocks around the tor.

27

4 5 6

1 2 3

← To Trewortha Tor

To Kilmar Tor & Bearah Tor

Back to the Car →

HAWK'S TOR (WESTERN END)

HAWK'S TOR (CAT'S HEAD ROCK)

(7) **Cat Nap**   25ft   *Severe 4b (AP)*   1960s
25ft right of the nose climb the centre of the main face, where
the rock is water worn, trending left to finish.

(8) **The Long Traverse**   20ft   *(6b) Boulder problem*
Reached from *Cat Nap*, or just right of it, traverse from the
left-side of the horizontal crack to the far right.

(9) **Up and over**   *(5c) Boulder problem.*
Move up to the lip of the roof via cracks and then pull over.

(10) **Hand Traverse**   *(5c)   Boulder problem.*
Left to right along the lip to its end then pull over the top.

Right of these tough problems, some 60ft along from Cat
Nap a detached block forms a chimney, beyond this the
South Face curves back into a recess.

(11) **Moss Chimney**   15ft   *Difficult 3c (AP)*   1941
Climb the chimney formed by the left-hand side of the block
and the face, followed by the short wall above.

(12) **Diagonal Crack**   12ft   *Difficult 3c (WP)*   1941
Mentioned really for historical continuity, this one move
wonder is the last climb before the break in the main ridge. At
the end of the shallow recess some 40ft right of *Moss Chimney*
the little left/right diagonal crack leads up onto the ridge at the
break immediately in front of the Cat's Head rock.

These next climbs are on the section of the South Face that
is slightly set back and has the highest outcrop of rock. On
the left of this outcrop, on the rim of the rock a catlike shape
can easily be seen. It appears to be looking back over its
shoulder, giving further credence to the belief that
the moors belong to large black felines.

(13) **The Cat's 'ere**   25ft   *Severe 4b (WP)*   1995
Move up the slab using the vertical layback and then move up
and left finishing by pulling on the cat's ear.

(14) **Pumping Panthers!**   30ft   *E3 6a (WP)*   ★1995
Start as for *The Cat's 'ere* moving up the slab by way of the

layback crack. At the roof traverse right along a rounded lip until a small crack in the lip is reached. This, then allows you to gain the top.

(15) **Big Black Pussy** 30ft *E2 6a (WP)* 1995

A few feet right of *Pumping Panthers* there is an obvious diagonal grey fault. Take this up the slab and through the roof to finish via a crack in the lip.

(16) **Rake and Flake** 25ft *Moderate 3c (WP)* 1941

10ft right again and this climb takes the vegetated left/right diagonal rake that leads to a scythe-like horizontal flake which sweeps out from the top boulder. Worth the scramble for the curious last move up from a comfortable seat in the flake!

(17) **Heather Chimney** 16ft *Moderate 3c (WP)* 1941

Right of the rake the outcrop rounds up and into a little, overgrown recess. This route is the way up through the back of the recess to the top of the tor. A couple of good moves means that it is not entirely without interest.

(18) **Black Beastie** 35ft *VS 4c (WP)* 1995

In the middle of the steep wall right of *Heather Chimney* climb a shallow crack to the small tree, then move right to pass through the fault in the lip and continue directly to the top.
Variation Start: E2 6a. 10ft to the right on the flat wall is a fault in the wall climb here until level with the tree then move left and continue as for *Black Beastie*.

(19) **Garden Chimney** 28ft *Moderate 3c (WP)* 1941

The very obvious easy chimney at the eastern end of the South Face, a few feet right of *Black Beastie's* variation start, it can be varied by climbing the inner route at the same grade. A pleasant climb.

(20) **Crack and Platform** 18ft *Moderate 3c (WP)* 1941

Similar to *Diagonal Crack* and nearly as pointless! Right at the east end of the ridge, scramble up a very short diagonal crack to round onto and up the ridge. A scrambler's way up rather than a walkers!

The next selection of climbs are found moving around the
West Buttress of the Cat's Head rock and onto the North

(21) **Chimney and Ledge**   24ft   *Difficult 4a (WP)*   1941

The climb starts just left of the West Buttress at the first obvious easy chimney/crack line. Climb up to the ledge on the left. Folkard's route moves left here to finish but a direct finish at V. Diff is better.

(22) **Fang Q**   30ft   *Severe 4a (WP)*   *1960s.

An obvious line up the large rounded break. To finish directly using a bucket hold over the lip.

(23) **Highly Clawsable**   30ft   *E4 6a (PP)*   1995

A much bolder proposition than the others. Start at the very base of the leftward trending fault. Do not follow the fault but climb directly up instead on very rounded and unprotected holds. Climb directly to the small break in the lip.

(24) **Jugular Vein**   35ft   *E1 5b (AP)*   1995

Start as for *Highly Clawsable*. Instead of climbing up follow the vein in its entirety. Although escapable at this point, refrain from stepping onto the grassy ledge. Continue on directly up to the large crack and the finish.

The face becomes short and broken here.

(25) **Mantle**   *(4c)*   *Boulder problem.*

Climb directly up the short face just left of *Highly Clawsable*.

(26) **Snatch & Mantle**   *(6a)*   *Boulder problem.*

A few yards left there is an obvious small overhang. It is a jump for the short, then a pull up on good sized holds gets you directly up onto the ridge.

Just to confuse the numbering system again! The last problem is located on the north side of the tor at its far western end, on the opposite side of the ridge to the TDK roof.

(27) **The Burn**   *(5b)*   Boulder problem.

A left to right traverse of this whole section.

Completing all the routes here will leave you dragging your knuckles in the mud like the proverbial Ape.

Despite having the highest hills and deepest quarries Bodmin Moor, north of the A30, remains the most neglected area in this guide. This is partly because the largest quarries; DeLank and Delabole are still being worked - and long walks are needed to explore potential bouldering areas. The South Moor is much more accessible but with the recent developments in sport climbing and the trend to document the tors for bouldering perhaps the North Moor may yet have its day. One of the most pleasing outings to be had in this area is a visit to the river valley crag of the Devil's Jump while there is plenty of high altitude bouldering on Rough Tor at 1311 feet.

ROUGH TOR

Landranger OS Sheet 200 GR 145807

A fine walk up gains you a splendid view of Cornwall's highest summit, Brown Willy, sadly bereft of rock. Rough Tor's top is very craggy but because of its remoteness has only been subject to casual attention until very recently. The rocks rise up to about 30ft with lots of scope for the boulderer who enjoys a walk.

HOW TO FIND

Just outside Camelford, heading north-east on the A39 towards Stratton, a right-hand turn takes you through Tregoodwell and onto Lower Moor. At the end of this road there is a car park below the tor. From the car park walk up and around the back of the main central tor. The wall containing the one recorded climb to date is on your left when facing back towards the car park.

THE CLIMB

The climb takes the largest bulging face that looks over to the top of Brown Willy.

Chicken in the Rough   30ft   *E5 6b (AP)*   ★1996

Immaculate grit style climbing. Climb the steep face directly by the horizontal breaks to gain the largest of these breaks. Here a small hold allows a long reach up the diagonal left to right fault line. Place a crucial 1.5 Friend before pulling up and finishing via a small fault in the lip.

THE DEVIL'S JUMP

A mini version of Devon's Dewerstone and a hidden gem. If you want a pleasant day out with a touch of adventure, then this is the place for you! A limited amount of bouldering can be found at this secluded outcrop, particularly in the small cave top left of the main crag, as well as a few good routes. One climb in particular has become recognised as the *crème de la crème* of V. Diff's. *The South East Climb* was originally described by Donald Romanis in 1921 as 'undoubtedly the finest inland climb in Cornwall'. It's still popular today, especially with the moorland explorer whose efforts will be well rewarded in seeking out this little treasure.

HOW TO FIND

From the Camelford (A39) to Wadebridge road, turn off onto the Bodmin road (B3266). Take the second left to Trecarne then turn right after half a mile, over the river Camel, to Henon Farm. Remember to ask permission to park. Follow the track for a short distance then scout around the hill on its right to the top of the tower.

THE CLIMBS

South East Climb   70ft   *Very Difficult (WP)*   ★★★1921
A smashing little route (I'm surprised Devon didn't take this one along with Downderry!). The front face of the tower is an imposing wall containing a line of overhangs. On its left flank is an obvious left leaning crack.
1: 35ft. Climb the crack to a stance on the shoulder.
2: 35ft. Climb the line of weakness in the wall on the right, with increasing exposure.

   The centre of the front wall provides a sustained route.

Beau Peep   80ft   *Hard Very Severe 5a (AP)*   1985
Climb the middle of the face via a thin crack to a break leading through the overlap. Continue in a direct line to the top.

South Face Route   80ft   *Very Severe 4c (AP)*   1975
Climb the right side of the face via a stepped rib, until it begins

to overhang, whereupon you can traverse left on big holds but in an exposed position. Finish right, up a rubble chimney.

East Face 40ft *HVS/E1 5a (AP)* 1974/85
On the overhanging black face, around to the right of the main face, the right-hand wall of the tower overhangs considerably. Climb this short but power-packed route directly up the leaning wall until better holds are reached leading to the top.

There are also some boulder problems on the small outcrop opposite The Devil's Jump.

HELMAN TOR *(Top section only)*

1
2
3
5c finish
4
5
6
7
8
9
10
12

HELMAN TOR

❌ *denotes top rope advised*

The diagram is not to scale and approximate! The numbers correspond to the numbers given to the boulder problems in the text. Some problems not mentioned in the text can be found on the diagram. The information is really only a rough guide to the best of a great bouldering area where many climbers have played for a great many years. Enjoy!

The Cave: great potential for gibbons! 6a, left hand cave wall & overhang on crimps.

p - denotes 'projects', not known to have yet been climbed.

Lip of the cave traversed from right to high slap exit, 6a

5b (the arete)
5a (the face)

Also problems on the hanging beam and in the cave.

6b Right side of bulging face.
5c Left side of face.

No Grieving

Also: hand traverse, feet up under, the roof (5b)

28

In the gutter

Stile

CAR PARK

Path

Stone wall

Dead End

13 — Battle of the Bulge

4a (crack)

14❌ – The Lip Gripper

Trig point

p12❌11
10 9 8 7❌ 6
2 1
3
4
5

16❌

Grassy Area

16a (Hell's Tooth)

17 (Bloody Helman)

Big Roof

Small cubic block

5b Mantel onto block.

5b Wall right of arete & mantel.

5b Right arete to long left hand reach & up.

4c Left arete.

22 – Crimping Crazy

21 20 19 18

25 24 23

Grassy bank

←To the square cut roof problem No15❌p

More problems can be found in the field opposite.
26 - Hanging Hancock and 27❌

Stile

Road

Fenced Area

5b/c Work through the roofs to crack and the top.

HELMAN TOR

Helman Tor offers a mass of quality bouldering, a small amount of short problem climbs and, at present, two actual routes. The rock is generally of good quality crystalline granite and has a very rough texture for the ultimate palming moves. The grass surrounding the boulder problems makes for soft landings in most cases. The options are widely varied, from friction to large roof problems, from painful crimping to jamming.

This site is being conserved and managed to encourage the establishment of heather and to maintain the diversity of ground flora and fauna which includes anemones and violets. The tor offers panoramic views of the surrounding valleys and the famous china clay area of Hensbarrow Down. The site is situated adjacent to archaeological remains of the Bronze Age settlement which is managed by English Heritage. Please remember that the beauty of places like this can so easily be destroyed by carelessness. Try to stay on the paths as much as possible and not trample on the surrounding vegetation. Keep brushing of holds to a minimum and resist the temptation to garden, there is plenty to climb here, without resorting to this unnecessary practice.

HOW TO FIND

From Plymouth take the A38 to Bodmin, turn left for the West Country onto the A30 and travel down the Bodmin bypass until you come to the roundabout. At the roundabout take the first left to Bugle and drive for approximately quarter of a mile and then turn down the first left you come to. Within 100 yards or so, turn right to Luxulyan. Now keep an eye open for a left turn to Helman Tor, when you find it go left for half a mile until you reach another left turn which is signposted to Helman Tor. Turn down here and travel for less than a mile until you see the rocks and the small right turn (with a sign post on the left and two granite posts either side of the turning on the right). Drive up this road and park in the car-park provided on the left.

THE CLIMBS

There are at present only two routes at this crag. As you enter the area from the car park look up and to your left. The lower section holds the highest and steepest wall. *Bloody Helman* can be found in the centre of this wall while the right rib gives:

(16a) **Hell's Tooth**   30ft   *E2 5c (AP)*   1995
Making a bold start, climb the rib in its entirety. Finish by stepping left and pulling over on good holds

(17) **Bloody Helman**   30ft   *E4 6a (AP)*   ★★1995
Another excellent short climb tucked away from the crowds. Climb the centre of the face direct, via two flakes and a small undercut to superb rounded finish.

THE BOULDER PROBLEMS

Starting on the higher crag; on the right in the back of the small bay the first problem is located on the back wall facing you. The problems are described from right to left.

1: ★6b. Climb directly from the horizontal crack, to a finger pocket and over the top.

2: 4a. Corner Crack.

3: 5c. Face only, from horizontal crack.

4: 3c. Large Crack.

5: 6a. Face with right-hand in crack.

6: 6b. Arete direct.

7: 6b. Left side wall, direct finish. Right finish goes at 5c.

8: 4c. Inside corner, move right to bucket finish.

9: ★5b. Thin crack only, direct finish via bucket.

10:★5a . Left side of the arete, layback groove finish.

11: 4a. Inside corner.

12: 6c+. Face only, direct.

13: ★6a. Bulge using obvious holds (no using side boulders).

14: ***6a. Up the ramp on the right and pull out onto the lip, traverse left to finish by pulling over roof.

15: *6b+. Left side out to the lip, around onto face and up.

16: 6a+. Layback the lower nose, direct finish.

16a. 5c The climb *Hell's Tooth* as described above.

17: 6a. The climb *Bloody Helman* as described above.

18: 3c. Directly up smooth ramp.

19: 5a. Pull up on flake, Mantel finish.

20: 5b. Direct small Mantel.

21: 6a. The arete, climbed on its right side using everything.

22: **6b. Left side of arete only.

23: 6a. Face only.

24: 5a. Up flakes direct.

25: 5c. Small rounded nose only, direct.

26: 5c. Left-side, pull through large bucket.

27: 6b+. Right-side via small flake.

28: 5c. Left to right hand traverse, Mantel finish.

TREFFRY VIADUCT

Legend has it you swim this way against the flow!

Blazey this

Car Park - Carnears Rocks & Lost World Quarry

Climb here

THE LUXULYAN VALLEY

Landranger OS Sheet 200 GR 056572

One mile north of St. Blazey this is Cornwall's answer to the Lost World. Sightings of pixies have been rumoured throughout this deeply wooded primeval valley! Hidden within its boundaries are a handful of huge boulders and crags, varying in quality from decent to incredibly kaolinized. One of the better quality outcrops is Carmears Rocks, the rock here is coarse, sharply crystalline, granite. A huge boulder made of a single granite block, once reputed to be the 'largest boulder in Europe,' is located at grid ref: 061576 and well worth a visit. The recorded climbs have a special character here.

HOW TO FIND

Take the Liskeard to St. Austell road (A390) as far as St. Blazey, cross the railway crossing and then turn right to Luxulyan. Continue for approximately half a mile until another right-hand turning for Luxulyan can be taken. Drive on for one mile until you reach the ten arch Treffry Viaduct, park here.

THE CLIMBS

The viaduct itself has been climbed. Legend has it by two short-sighted climbers who, travelling west, thought they had reached Land's End and were on the Atlantic Ocean Wall; the similarity is easy to see! One of them, (he shall remain nameless) on reaching the top, discovered the covered leat that runs hidden within the length of the viaduct. Believing this to be Flambard's water slide, he dived on in.

Treffry Viaduct   90ft   *E3 5c (AP)*   1991

Why? Is there a lack of rock in Cornwall!? Climb the South Face of the leg on the left (between the road and the river) as you look north. Moving up and right over the arch as height and the top are gained.

Captain Webb   750ft   *Ex. Stupid (PP)*   1991

Rubber up for this one! Swim, crawl, dive and panic your way up stream along the length of this high altitude under water labyrinth. Beware, parts have become narrowed over the years

LUXULYAN, TREFFRY VIADUCT & QUARRY

Woodland footpath follows leat, passing a ruined water wheel to Carmears Rocks (approx 20 minutes walk)

Car Park

Captain Webb

Lower path to Carmear's Rocks

Quarry
Scamble up

Treffry Viaduct

Luxulyan approx ¾ mile

2
1

Parking

The numbers on the maps correspond to the numbers for the climbs given in the text. **Note:** The climbs on Carmears Rocks do not follow a strict left to right rule being described (loosely) in the order that people encounter the rocks as they work their way up the heavily wooded hillside.

St. Blazey 1 mile approx.

CARMEARS ROCKS

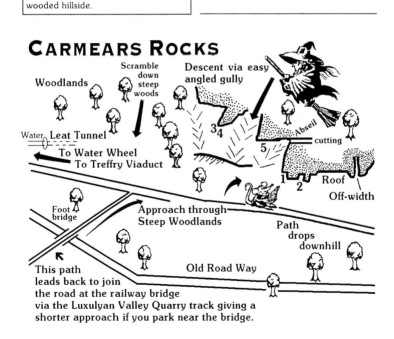

Woodlands

Scramble down steep woods

Descent via easy angled gully

Water Leat Tunnel

To Water Wheel
To Treffry Viaduct

3
4

5

Abseil

cutting

1
2
Roof
Off-width

Foot bridge

Approach through Steep Woodlands

Path drops downhill

This path leads back to join the road at the railway bridge via the Luxulyan Valley Quarry track giving a shorter approach if you park near the bridge.

Old Road Way

by all types of junk which may including the bodies of those who have followed in the footsteps of our gallant leader, Captain Webb (see first ascents for identity).

Editor's Note: A bizarre example of modern climbers exploiting their climbing skills in the cause of exploring Cornwall's industrial heritage *Captain Webb* is not a recommended route. Previous generations have been too embarrassed to claim such escapades but Hell! This is the nineties, have you taken the Pepsi Challenge yet?

CARMEARS ROCKS

GR 069564

Among the many hidden rocks and outcrops to be found in the valley are Carmears Rocks which have a coarse and rather sharp crystalline type of granite. They were explored for climbing by Donald Romanis as long ago as 1921 but forgotten again until quite recently. In his day the area was dominated by the workings of Pont's Mill and a wooden trough carried the leat across the face of the main rocks. Water would cascade from this for 200ft down the valley side and was a popular local attraction. Romanis recorded ascents here of *The Waterfall Slabs* – the main climb on these was 'essentially not a boulder problem' and meandered up the slabby area, to the right of the steep main rocks, for over 100ft. The area is now overgrown and heavily wooded.

HOW TO FIND

Leave the viaduct and follow the leat (water course) south, passing the remains of an old waterwheel. Descend the incline until a track leads left, the rocks can be seen high on the left after a few hundred yards.

THE CLIMBS

The crag is divided into two distinct areas. The main buttress on the right and the pinnacles high on the left. At present two routes exist on the main buttress which is the first cliff reached as you climb the heavily vegitated hillside.

(1) **Titch**   40ft   *Hard Severe 4a (AP)*   1989
Take the large crack/groove on the left of the buttress finishing just right of an oak tree.

(2) **Game On**   40ft   *E2 5c (WP)*   1995

The thin crack through the overlap just right of *Titch*, hard move into the crack above the break.

Three routes exist on the pinnacle, from left to right.

(3) **Aretion**   60ft   *Hard Severe 4a (AP)*   1995

Take the left-hand arete, starting by an iron pole. Climb up right to an oak tree and move left onto the arete which is followed to the top.

(4) **Hullabaloo**   60ft   *VS 4c (AP)*   1995

Start as for *Aretion*, but at the tree move up right into the fine crack which leads to the top.

(5) **Drippy & Strangely Brown**   70ft   *Hard Very Severe 5a (AP)*   1989

The right-hand pinnacle starting at the base of the easy gully left of the main buttress. Take the wall past a peg runner where devious moves make it easier to gain the ledge above. Move on up the arete on its slabbed left-side to perched blocks at the top.

LUXULYAN VALLEY QUARRY ——

GR 059568

500 yards south of Treffry viaduct you can park near the railway bridge. A two minute walk, along the track beside the railway, leads around into the quarry which is on the east side of the road.

THE CLIMBS

The farthest wall in the quarry gives two hard climbs.

(1) **My Life Led Up To This**   60ft *F7a+ (E4 6b) (WP)*   1995

Is situated on the left side of the blank wall at the back of the quarry. Climb up and on to a slim ledge. Use the second bolt for aid, then move left and up the groove to finish.

(2) **Strongbow**   60ft   *F7c (E6 6b/c) (WP)*   ★★★1996

This excellent climb requires superior finger strength. Start 10 feet right of *'My Life...'* and climb the obvious bow shaped fault that thins as it rises to a small ledge and a bolt lower-off. Or, a loose finish to the top.

THE LOST WORLD QUARRY

Now, this place really does hold that feeling of enchantment. Especially when viewed from the rim of the quarry. Best to study the map to locate it. It has a feeling of peace and tranquillity which comes rushing to meet you (especially after a tinny or two). The brambles at the base of the quarry however, bring back memories of the film *20,000 Leagues Under the Sea* as their tentacle-like arms grapple with your torso. The approach is even more delightful, this can only be likened to a major jungle expedition, but then that's half the fun of these places. There are at present only two climbs here. However, to make you feel better, they are of good quality on sound rock but be discreet and considerate as the quarry is on private land.

HOW TO FIND

From the viaduct, head towards Luxulyan village, take the first right up a narrow lane (car park on the right, park here.) As you walk up the hill you will cross a leat, just past this take the track on the left through an old iron gate. Walk for half a mile along this path until you enter the Quarry, the routes are at the far end.

THE CLIMBS

The climbs are described from right to left. Starting at the arete.

On Mirkwood Edge   60ft   *E4 6b (AP)*   ★★1991
Climb the steep arete on the right of the furthest face, at the back of the Quarry. One peg runner, and tree branch for protection to start otherwise climb direct.

Bouncy Bouncy Kangaroo   60ft   *E5 6b (WP)*   ★★1995
The central fault line up the large blank looking wall left of *On Mirkwood Edge*, bolts and peg runners insitu.

Editor's Note: Visitors to the Luxulyan quarries will notice bolts etc., not on the climbs described. At the time of writing these are 'sport projects' still awaiting redpoint ascents.

ROCHE ROCK

The numbers correspond to the numbers of the climbs given in the text.

Note. The West Face is easy, broken and vegetated and under no circumstance should it be 'gardened.'

Natural protection, nut and cam placements abound. Pitons and bolts must never be used at Roche and, there is no need!

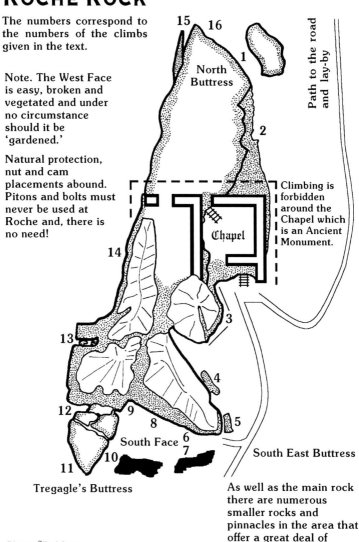

Climbing is forbidden around the Chapel which is an Ancient Monument.

Path to the road and lay-by

North Buttress

Chapel

South Face

South East Buttress

Tregagle's Buttress

Diagram ©Toni Carver

As well as the main rock there are numerous smaller rocks and pinnacles in the area that offer a great deal of pleasant bouldering.

ROCHE ROCK

Roche Rock, which rises about 70 feet from flat surrounding moorland, near the village of Roche, is regarded as one of the best examples of tourmalinization. The rock consists of quartz-schorl, a type of altered granite in which the feldspar and mica have been replaced by tourmaline. It makes the hard, firm rock with its weird and wonderful pockets very pleasing to climb on. The edges of the rock are very rounded, but feel rough. In places thin fins can be found. Many of the pockets are deeper than they look and are often full of crystals.

Drama is added by St. Michael's Chapel. This ancient building, built on the rock in the fourteenth century, was the home of local monks. Later it was the habitation of a hermit, said to have suffered from leprosy. Living alone, within these desolate walls, must have been very boring. Which is one of the reasons why I believe he probably enjoyed the climbing that is on offer here. Proof of this can still be found in several finger pockets!

Roche Rock and its monastery are an ingredient of Cornwall's magical aura. The giant Tregagle, who for a terrible misdeed was tasked by the Devil to drain Dozmary Pool with a limpet shell, ran away and stuck his head through the chapel window seeking sanctuary. But he couldn't get inside and the Devil chased him over the moors howling in terror with a pack of hell hounds at his heels! In a bad gale the wind is said to 'howl like Tregagle' locally. These weird aspects of Roche Rock are probably why it was used as a location for the film 'Omen III'. Spend a night here and see what you think of all those silly old ghost stories!

Roche Rock is part of Lord Falmouth's estate. The public are allowed access and the chapel ruins are classified as an ancient monument. Climbing on the chapel walls is not permissible and all the climbs give them a wide berth, nor is removal of the vegetation from the surrounding rocks. The quality of the rock and superb standard of protection means that pitons (let alone bolts) are not required and must never be placed under any circumstances. It should be noted that any damage to this crag would constitute a serious act of trespass, doubtless leading to a prosecution.

One of South East Cornwall's traditional crags Roche was first described by Donald Romanis in 1921. Far more climbing has been done here than has ever been recorded; the result of changing attitudes! An ideal soloing venue, from the 1970's onward Roche has usually been regarded as a stop-off for some fast training. As a result the climbs recorded really only represent a matrix of good routes around which good climbers have often been witnessed doing far harder and more impressive variations.

HOW TO FIND

From the A30 turn South for the village of Roche which is located below the clay mounds, near St. Austell. St. Michael's Chapel is situated upon the rock and is easily seen when approaching Roche. From the village roundabout carry on past the pub then turn left for Bugle. The Rock with its Chapel are within 500 yards on the right.

THE CLIMBS

The climbs start at the short fierce looking overhang, which can be seen when walking up to the crag below the narrow North Buttress. The climbs are described from right to left around the rock, returning to the original starting point.

(1) God Forbid   65ft   E4 6b (AP) ★★1994

A brilliant grit style problem, takes on the actual overhang. Climb the obvious overhang, using the crack and right-hand pocket to gain the precarious sloping ledge. Move on directly up the arete to a vertical crack in a shallow groove to finish.

To the left of the powerful overhang which undercuts the North Buttress Arete the crag rounds onto the East Face. A climb remembered as 'Hook and Eye' was said to work its way through the bulges just left of 'God Forbid' at about Very Severe but we have no other details of this climb which was the product of the Rob Bennett and Rob Walker era when much was done but little recorded!
The steep wall between here and the Chapel has two very distinct groove lines in it. Do not climb on the Chapel walls which in any case are well clear of the lines.

(2) **East Chimney** 65ft *Severe 4b (AP)* 1921

A steep corner a few yards left of *God Forbid* gains the water worn groove on the left which is followed to the top. This line provides the basis for other variations on the wall. The right-hand groove, more impressive and harder, has so far escaped both claiming and naming! But, ascents have been recollected.

Moving left past the Chapel itself, the well worn footpath reaches the iron ladder which leads into the chapel providing an easy way to the top of the rock.

(3) **Oxford Climb** 45ft *Very Difficult 4a (AP)* 1933

From the top of the iron ladder traverse left around an awkward bulge to gain a crack which slants back right.

A deep, vegetated gully divides the bulging wall of Oxford Climb from the South East Buttress where the climbs are quite close to each other.

(4) **Ivy-Mantled Tower** 50ft *Severe 4b (AP)* ★1955

About 15ft left of the iron ladder a large ivy covered block leans up against the buttress, another smaller cleaner rock, within bridging distance, to the left also abuts the buttress. Bridge up, first between the two rocks, then between the right-hand rock and the face until good holds in a groove on the face are gained. Strong climbing, trending slightly right, leads directly up the face to the top.

(5) **South East Buttress** 65ft *Difficult 4a (AP)* ★★1921

The best of the earliest recorded climbs in South East Cornwall and a true archetype. Start 20ft left of the chapel ladder and climb to the top of the smaller rock to good holds on the buttress. The left-hand of two narrow grooves at 15ft is followed up and around to emerge high on the South Face where a 15ft traverse left leads to a crack which slants back right and leads to the top.

Variation. From a good knob at the top of the groove climb directly to the top thus avoiding the traverse and the climb's classic feel!

Rounding the buttress brings you into a pleasant bay formed by the South Face of the rock and the adjoining 20ft high Tregagle's Buttress to its left.

(6) **Moping Owl**   60ft   *Very Severe 4c (AP)*   ★1955

At the right-hand end of the South Face an obvious crack curves right at 15ft. Follow this up, and around, until it is possible to reach a huge hold on the wall above. Use this to start a sensational, swingy hand-traverse right, around the nose of the South East Buttress, to gain a stance on the far side. A step up allows a return to the South Face where the climb then finishes vertically.

(7) **Porky**   50ft   *Very Severe 4c (AP)*   ★★★1974

The direct variation of the previous line. Start as for *Moping Owl* and climb the crack directly for 15ft then the short corner and overhang above by pulling directly into the 'lava' groove. Follow this and the short slab above to the top of the buttress.

(8) **The Lord Falmouth**   55ft   *E1 5b/c (PP)*   ★★Rec.1997

This excellent direct line up the South Face takes the centre of the slab between *Moping Owl* and *Corner & Staircase*. Climb the slab trending right where a technical confidence move (trust your feet!) leads to the curving crack and huge hand hold of *Moping Owl*. Mantel up over this and climb the slab, overlap and pinnacle block above to exit on the highest point of the crag. There is no protection before the crux.

On the left side of the small bay is an easy corner which gives.

(9) **Corner & Staircase**   45ft   *Difficult 3b (AP)*   1921

Climb the corner and prominent crack on the left-hand side of the South Face then gallop up the blocks that lead up to the chapel ruins. The climbers path up the rock!

(10) **Tregagle's Crack**   25ft   *Severe 4b (WP)*   1921

On the left wall of the bay is a hand sized crack. Start this with difficulty, climbing becomes easier as the crack widens with height and the top of the small Tregagle's Buttress is gained. Join *Staircase* or descend the *Corner*.

(11) **Tregagle's Buttress**   20ft   *Hard Severe 4b/c(AP)*   1921

Bold for its day even though combined tactics were used on the first ascent. The front (south face) of the little buttress still stands as a challenge to today's E-men and has not been climbed! The climb starts around just left of the south west arete and takes a bold and interesting sequence of moves on intriguing holds to the top of the buttress.

(12) **Easy Chimney**   50ft *Difficult 3c (PP)*   1921
This wide chimney is part of the fissure that separates Tregagle's Buttress from the main rock (West Face) on the opposite side to *Corner & Staircase*. Chimney up or use very wide bridging moves, to the top of the buttress. It is also possible to squeeze through the back of the fissure. After the chimney continue up *Staircase* or carry on squeezing between the pinnacles above which lead to the chapel floor.

"A pleasant route up the rock, suitable for any ladies who should happen to be members of the picnic party," as Donald Romanis remarked!

(13) **Swink Chimney**   55ft   *Very Severe 4c (PP)*   1955
About 8ft left of *Easy Chimney* a steep narrow second chimney is gained at 10ft from a bulging start. It finishes on ledges at 20ft. From here walk up and left about 15ft to a steep groove with an overhanging start which is climbed boldly to the top.

(14) **Tump Wall**   50ft   *Difficult 3c (AP)*   1955
The large expanse of vegetated wall left of *Swink Chimney*. Climb the wall by a direct line of vegetated grooves in its centre. Easy and disappointing.

Continuing around the vegetated wall until you are almost back at the start. The overhang should now be on your left and a large groove is visible to your right.

(15) **North Buttress**   50ft   *Difficult 3c (AP)*   1921
This climb takes the large groove just to the right. Climb to a boulder at the top. Then move back and up the wall above the groove. It is also possible to traverse left onto the nose from the North Buttress.

(16) **Shorty's Folly**   55ft   *Very Severe 4c (AP)*   ★1971
Start at the foot of the North Buttress. Climb straight up the wall to a ledge. Finish up the obvious fault line in the centre of the face.

(16a) Variation Finish   *Hard Severe 4c (AP)*   1971
A finish up the groove to the left will reduce the climb's danger grade.

> *Besides these main climbs boulder problems abound, and
> many small routes have been left unrecorded. These
> are for you to rediscover at your leisure on a lazy
> summer's afternoon. But remember to leave
> before dark, or at least carry a clove of
> garlic and a bloody great cross
> or you could find yourself
> howling like Tregagle!*

ROCHE ROCK & ST. MICHAEL'S CHAPEL

Viewed from the road side - North Buttress & East Face -
Numbers shown correspond to the numbers
given for the climbs in the text.

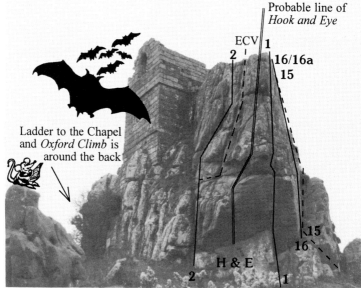

2, *East Chimney* can be varied on the right (ECV).

The South Coast

Landranger OS Sheets 201, 200 & 204

The coastline covered by this guidebook stretches from the mouths of the rivers Tamar in the East to the Fal in the South West. Climbing venues, from Rame Head to Nare Head. Climbers have been exploring these areas since the 1920s but, because of the very mixed quality of rock, development has been intermittent although often spectacular climbs have resulted.

Rame Head

Sheet 201 GR 417487

Legend has it that there are some half a dozen routes on shale up to 150ft high in the west side of the head. Only worth a visit if you are in the area.

Downderry Beach

GR 330538

'Devon get your thieving hands off!' This crag belongs to South East Cornwall. Our hot little treasure has some of the best workout bouldering available in Cornwall or Devon. This is thanks to the smooth overhanging nature of the rock. It tends not to leave you screaming in agony every time you pick up your coffee by the mug, instead of the handle.

The bouldering is nearly all overhanging, with sand to soften the numerous landings. In certain areas, however, it is advisable to treat the rock with care. If not, you'll find yourself with a variety of holds to show your friends when you get home. There is a nudist preserve at the far end of the beach which can prove a distraction.

HOW TO FIND

From Plymouth (A38), take a left at Trerulefoot roundabout (A374) to Polbathic. Turn right before Polbathic (A387) to Hessenford. Turn left in the centre of the village, opposite the Copley Arms towards Seaton (B3247). Carry on through Seaton and then on through Downderry, but not as far as the hairpin bends.

Park on the left in a small bay or up the left turn to Bottlegate Close and walk up to the first hairpin. Here it is possible to find a public footpath on the right. On entering the path immediately turn right down an overgrown path. The main climbing can be found within 400 yards, although there is an array of bouldering all along the beach which is tidal so check the tide timetable.

THE BOULDERING

The bouldering extends all along the beach. Here are just a few of the main problems to start you off. It is worth noting that after a storm sand can ruin some of the bouldering. In particular The Wave which becomes buried and the cave loses its sandy landing, making it dangerous.

The Wave   35ft   *6b* ★★★

Usually started on the far right and traversed to the very end on the left. 'Plenty of excellent hand slapping moves!' (Must be due to the company.)

Move right, around the corner to the next overhanging wall.

The Undercut   20ft   *6b*

Traverse from the right to the left, the hardest moves are in the middle.

*Turn to the outcrop that shoots out towards the sea
Start at the landward end.*

The Promontory   40ft   *5c* ★★

Climb up at the landward end and traverse out to the far end. Hard move at half distance.

Having walked around the promontory you will find a cave. The right-hand wall has a crack running all the way back its full length.

DOWNDERRY BEACH (not to scale!)

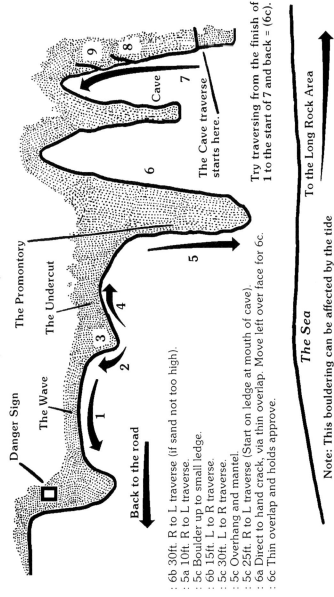

: 6b 30ft. R to L traverse (if sand not too high).
: 5a 10ft. R to L traverse.
: 5c Boulder up to small ledge.
: 6b 15ft. L to R traverse.
: 5c 30ft. L to R traverse.
: 5c Overhang and mantel.
: 5c 25ft. R to L traverse (Start on ledge at mouth of cave).
: 6a Direct to hand crack, via thin overlap. Move left over face for 6c.
: 6c Thin overlap and holds approve.

Note: This bouldering can be affected by the tide

141

DOWNDERRY CAVE

DOWNDERRY BEACH

The Cave 30ft *5c*★★★

Start on the right of the cave mouth on top of the rock that juts out of the side wall. Swing down on to the rounded holds and continue on in. At half distance move up into the break and continue. If you have the strength try and return.

Try the two cracks that run up the wall. The first is 6b and the second is 6c. The left side of the cave also has a large selection of excellent problems and the whole cave can be traversed at 6b. To the right of the cave the flying buttress can be traversed left to right at 6b and there is more climbing down the beach.

LONG ROCK (DOWNDERRY)

Moving to the far end of the beach where an obvious rock juts out of the sea. Via a system of easy rock hopping at low tide, the landward side of the rock can be obtained. It is then possible to scramble around to the right and the back to gain the top. Though why anyone would want to is beyond me, as it stinks of seagull guano!

THE CLIMBS

The climbs described start on the right (looking out to sea) and move around to the left (landward) and around the corner to the east side of the rock.

(1) **Long Rock Climb** 50ft *Very Difficult 4b (PP)* circa 1991
Climb around to the right side (looking out to sea) of the rock at low tide. Just after rounding the corner start to climb the face.

(2) **Fang Arete** 50ft *E3 5b (PP)* 1991
Jump onto the landward side of the stack. Then climb directly up and out to the right, then climb the landward side of the arete.

(3) **The Fang Direct** 50ft *E2 5b (PP)* 1991
Jump on to the landward side of the stack. Climb the centre of the face to gain the groove and then climb this in its entirety. Loose rock at the top.

(4) **La De Dah**   50ft   *Severe 4b* (AP)   1995

Climb around the left side of the rock at low tide for approximately 12ft then move up the face by the easiest and most obvious line.

LONG ROCK CLIFF

Moving away east from the rock altogether and returning to the cliff face. Over to the right some 50ft from the Long Rock you will find a low overhung cave.

(5) **Shlong**   40ft   *Hard Severe 4b (PP)*   circa 1991

Start just right of the cave. Climb up and right, then back left up the steep wall / groove to the slab above. Belays up and left.

Right again is a corner groove capped by an overhang at half height.

(6) **Infelation**   40ft *Hard Very Severe 5a (PP)* circa 1991

Climb the corner, move out right and over the overhang. Now climb the slab on the left to gain the continuation groove to the top.

Right again there is a platform at approximately 15ft. There are two routes here.

(7) **The Queen of Rock**   40ft *Severe 4b (PP)* circa 1991

The rib left of the corner can be climbed directly.

(8) **Left Feeling a Little Queer**   40ft *Hard Severe 4b (PP)* circa 1991

To the right is yet another rib. This can also be climbed directly.

THE COAST: TALLAND BAY TO POLRUAN

The Jerram and Romanis families lived at Talland Bay and Bertrand and Donald were friends from childhood. Perhaps not surprisingly, with the limitations on transport, this loose stretch of coastline was their 'local crag.' Donald Romanis, in particular, spent many hours bouldering and scrambling here. Perhaps not surprisingly, given the ease of transport and the poor quality of the rock, the area holds little appeal for today's climbers; unless it's a beach day with the family.

TALLAND BAY

OS Sheet 201 GR 222510

On the west side of Talland Bay, Landslip Cove offered at least two good scrambling 'courses' back in the 1920s. These were situated on the south side of the cove where it is bordered by a ridge and the best climbs are located on the north face of the ridge. Romanis' 'Circular Climb' was essentially a bouldering traverse down, around and over the north and south faces of the ridge. This area has plenty of loose cliffs which are not popular although the beaches are.

SMUGGLERS' COVE

OS Sheet 201 GR. 216507

Half a mile east of Polperro, Smuggler's cove offers climbing 'of a sort' on both its east and west buttresses while the high cliff to the West gives a dangerous 200ft loose route. A note of Donald Romanis' from 1920 reads. *"It would appear to be possible to climb the cliff at the back of the cove direct, but at present this has never been attempted and the loose nature of the rock renders it unjustifiable — except for a climber who wishes to break his neck"*. Still the case in 1998, as none seem to have risen to the challenge!

CHAPEL CLIFF, POLPERRO

OS Sheet 201 GR 210507

Scrambling and one climb of historical interest which is located on the south side of the 'peak', immediately above the Chapel Pool.

Chapel Chimney 40ft Difficult 1920
Climb this very lonely chimney with the difficulty reserved for the last 8 feet.

Between Blackbottle Rocks and Chapel Cliff Romanis noted plenty of scrambling on very unreliable rock.

PENCARROW HEAD

The numbers on the diagram correspond to the numbers given to the climbs in the text.

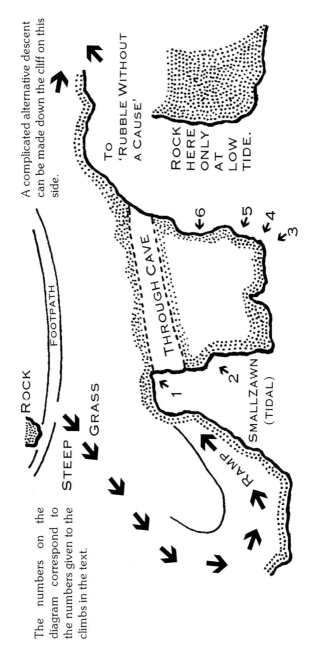

A complicated alternative descent can be made down the cliff on this side.

TO 'RUBBLE WITHOUT A CAUSE'

ROCK HERE ONLY AT LOW TIDE.

ROCK

FOOTPATH

STEEP

GRASS

THROUGH CAVE

RAMP

SMALLZAWN (TIDAL)

1

2

3

4

5

6

Sean Hawken on Rubble Without a Cause (E4 5c) Pencarrow Head.   *Photo: Andy Grieve*

147

Nick Hancock on Splitting Images (E2 5c) Dodman Point.　*Photo: Pete Saunders*

PENCARROW HEAD

Pencarrow Head forms the eastern boundary of Lantic Bay. Previously only limited scrambling on Devonian slates was noted so the headland appears, at first glance, to have little to offer. Recently, however, it has become a favourite haunt for some local climbers. So, what does Pencarrow have to offer? Well, the answer is a great deal of fun if you're into deep water soloing (high tide is best). However, when it comes to actual climbs this place still has the usual looseness with the same intimidating characteristics found on the rest of the South Cornwall Coast. Due to this, the headland, despite its large amount of rock, offers only a handful of climbs and these generally tend to have an adventuresome air about them.

HOW TO FIND

The roads are fairly well sign posted for this one, however, if you have a map it would be advisable to make use of it. Pass Liskeard on the A38 to Dobwalls. Pick up the A390 (St Austell) for approximately two miles and then turn left on to the B3359 (Pelynt). Follow this until it is possible to turn right (Polruan), then follow the signs to the small village of Polruan. About two miles before Polruan and on the right you will discover the car park for Pencarrow Head, park here. From the car park walk towards Polruan for 100 yards and then step over the stile on the left and cross the field. At the end of the field pass through a gate (this area is owned by the National Trust) and walk — not down to the beach, but — directly onward to the headland. The main attraction (the deep water soloing) is found by an investigative descent down the steep grass to a small zawn with an overhanging wall. More soloing and some of the climbing is then found by scrambling east under a section of the cliff via a 'through cave.'

THE CLIMBS

Warning: all the climbs have soft and loose rock so treat all insitu gear (even if in good condition) with caution. Being a competent swimmer is also a must for deep water soloing! All the routes require some traversing, or a swim to reach the starts.

The Go Between   60ft   *Hard Very Severe 5a (AP)*   1996

At the entrance to the 'through cave' there is an obvious crack (leading to a large thread) climb up the wall and onto the roof of the cave. Traverse the slabby face by following the arching crack line. It is possible to then carefully scramble to the top.

After passing through the 'through cave', you will find another small zawn. The climbs are on the right of this zawn (as you look out to sea) and are described from left to right. The following routes were all climbed as deep water solos, however, they have been graded for low tide ascents.

The Long Drop   35ft   *Hard Very Severe 5b*   1996

The seaward arete. Climb directly up the rounded arete. Descend just to the left via an easy chimney or carefully scramble to the top.

Grim Reefer   35ft   *E1 5b (PP)*   1996

The best line on this little face. From the small ledge at sea level follow the thin crack line to the top. Descend to the left via an easy chimney or carefully scramble to the top of the headland.

In Cod We Trust   30ft   *Hard Very Severe 5a (AP)*   1996

From the small ledge at sea level climb the large broken crack line to the top. Descend to the left via the easy chimney or carefully scramble to the top of the headland.

Captain Birdseye   30ft   *Very Severe 5c (PP)*   1996

Move approximately 10ft right of the large crack, and once more from the small ledge at sea level follow the very thin crack line until it is possible to break left and finish at the same point as *In Cod We Trust*. Descend to the left via an easy chimney or carefully scramble to the top of the headland.

Moving approximately 100 yards farther along the coast (toward the inner coastline of Lantivet Bay). On the bend of the path descend the steep slope to the cliff edge. Move right around the overhanging cliff face and then down-climb the cliff to the top of a sloping platform. The next climb makes a rising traverse along the obvious fault line of the overhanging wall.

Rubble Without A Cause   100ft   *E4 5c (AP)*   1996

A really superb looking route but the rock is delicate! Start from the left and traverse right passing two insitu pegs along the obvious rising bannister. From the angled ledge pull up via a very loose flake and then swing wildly up onto the next angled platform, finish up the short steep face.

BLACKBOTTLE ROCKS

OS Sheet 200 GR 136504

Between Lantic Bay and the mouth of the Fowey there are intermittent outcrops of grey slate projecting from the cliff at intervals, offering some mediocre climbing. Blackbottle Rocks on the western side of Lantic Bay, are a little more interesting.

BLACK HEAD

OS Sheet 204 GR 041479

Black Head is located in St. Austell Bay between Charlestown and Mevagissey. There are some boulder problems but still only one recorded climb which is to be found in the large zawn facing south on the headland.

Black Jack   120ft   *Very Severe 4c (PP)*   1972

Start beneath the overhanging wall on the obvious traverse line in the 'brown band' at sea level.

1: 70ft 4c. Traverse right for 20ft, step down and then up to the corner to traverse right again, delicate. An aid move gains the chimney which is followed past a large chockstone to a ledge and belay.

2: 50ft, 4c. Another aid move, left off the ledge, leads to a large sloping ledge. Follow cracks past overhangs and ledges to the top and belay well back.

Editor's Note: The 4c technical grade was tagged onto a very short description of *Black Jack* in the *Climbers' Club North Devon and Cornwall Guide* of 1988, consequently there may be some confusion as to the exact line. It is the original description published here, and although the aid moves can probably now be dispensed with no aid elimination has actually been recorded.

DODMAN POINT

Or as the Cornish like to say "Dead man Point."

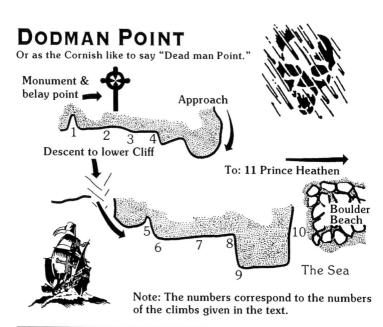

Monument & belay point

Approach

1 2 3 4

Descent to lower Cliff

To: 11 Prince Heathen

Boulder Beach

5 6 7 8 9 10

The Sea

Note: The numbers correspond to the numbers of the climbs given in the text.

NARE HEAD

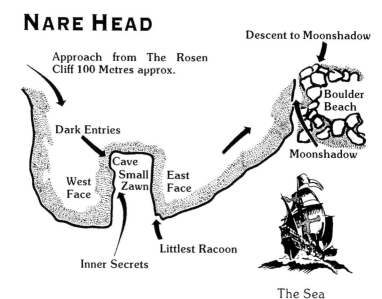

Approach from The Rosen Cliff 100 Metres approx.

Descent to Moonshadow

Dark Entries

Boulder Beach

Cave Small Zawn

West Face

East Face

Moonshadow

Littlest Racoon

Inner Secrets

The Sea

DODMAN POINT

Located on the coast almost due south of St. Austell, the views are charming and panoramic from Dodman Point. There is a considerable amount of rock on this headland which at 373ft is unusually high for the South Coast. On top of the headland there is an unmistakable monument. Parts of the Dodman are impressively steep but the rock consists of schist, a metamorphic rock characterised by brittle, often wafer-thin layers. The rock quality, therefore, ranges from solid, through friable to downright loose. This makes it an exciting and challenging place to climb.

HOW TO FIND

Find the hamlet of Penare. Park in the car park, then walk south along the footpath until you reach the monument. To the left of the monument it is possible to walk around the face and gain the foot of the upper face. A steep gully then provides a convenient descent to the lower section of the cliff. From the foot of the descent gully the main cliffs extend to the north east. The first main feature is a big 150ft wall with the obvious corner of Horrorshow.

THE CLIMBS ON THE UPPER CLIFF.

The climbs are described from left to right when your back is to the sea.

(1) Garfield's Gut   50ft   *Difficult 4a (PP)*   1986
Close to the left-hand descent and set slightly back is a slanting chimney. Climb the chimney.

Fifty yards right of Garfield's Gut is a slab with a diagonal break.

(2) Splitting Images   60ft   *E2 5c (AP)*   1986
Climb the left side of the slab via a vague line of weakness. Finish with difficulty up a thin crack (two peg runners). The stone cross makes for a safe belay.

(3) **In God We Trust**   60ft   *E3 5b (PP)*   1991

Climb directly up the slab (peg runner) right of Splitting Images and belay using the cross for the ultimate protector.

(4) **Divine Comedy**   90ft   *E1 5a (PP)*   1996

Climb the slab by the right to left diagonally rising break. Crumbling rock and poor gear make for an interesting time! At the end of the break, climb up and slightly right to gain the top.

THE CLIMBS ON THE LOWER CLIFF

(5) **Horrorshow**   150ft   *E4 6a (PP)* ★1973

A serious undertaking with very strenuous climbing which takes a superb line up the obvious incut corner in the main wall.

1: 100ft 6a. Follow the corner past a bulge to a second overhang at 40ft formed by a flake on the right wall. Move out and climb the flake crack to the main overhang which is passed by hard strenuous climbing. Move up to flat holds above the final roof and make a steep pull to stand on them. Traverse left to a stance in a grassy hollow (originally a peg belay).

2: 50ft. Climb the groove and pleasant slabs above.

Move on further around to the east. The wall here is split impressively by a crack. To the left of the crack is the following route.

(6) **Dod on Arrival**   50ft   *Exceptionally Severe 5b (PP)*   1991

A serious undertaking, the rock is very friable. The left side of the wall is climbed by the easiest possible route. The exact line is unclear.

(7) **Sex Tips For Monogamous Girls**   150ft   *E3 5b (PP)*   1989

A superb looking climb taking the obvious major crack in the centre of the wall that splits it in two.

(8) **Snap Happy**   60ft   *E3 5b (PP)*   1989

The corner right of *Sex Tips For Monogamous Girls* is climbed direct. On the first ascent the pegs were placed on the lead and removed 'by hand' by the second as he climbed.

(9) Jood The Zood 90ft *E3 5b (PP)* 1986
Start 30ft right of *Snap Happy* below the right bounding arete.
Climb to the right to gain a ledge. Move back left and follow
the arete to the top. Exposed and with minimal protection.

Moving around to the opposite side of the buttress. There is
one more route in the centre of the wall.

(10) Un-named 85ft *Very Severe 4b (PP)* 1972
Climb the crack, which is loose and serious in its upper
section, to belay on the ridge on the right.

The cliff becomes broken for a few hundred yards. Walk
over until a second buttress with a huge corner is reached.
There is one route on this buttress at present.

(11) Prince Heathen 150ft *Very Severe 4b/c (PP)* 1972
Start 5ft right of the arete of the corner on the steep wall.
Climb easily on good sound holds to a ledge at 70ft. The slab
above is more difficult and is ascended just right of a
grass-filled crack. After 50ft steep grass is encountered and
the search for a belay should begin.

THE NARE HEAD AREA

OS sheet 204 GR 923373

Nare Head is the large headland between Dodman Point and
Falmouth Harbour, large and impressive the head itself is
disappointing due to very loose rock. However, the area has
some of the best climbing on the South Coast which is situated
in a small zawn between the head and Kiberick Cove (GR
925380) about a kilometre and a half to the north-east.

In the 1920s Donald Romanis noted several long scrambles on
the western rocks of Nare Head proper. His most impressive
ascent being the great nose of rock at the extreme point of the
head. Starting at sea level up a crack line the climb finishes
below the south-east corner of the nose. However, for most
modern climbers the Head offers only a handful of short
problems.

HOW TO FIND

Not the easiest place to find despite being owned by the National Trust. The roads are not well signposted but the village of Veryan can be found tucked away amongst the typically narrow lanes of Cornwall. It is advisable to make use of the map. Once you have stumbled upon the village, in all of its Dark Age glory, it should be possible to discover the car park above Kilberick Cove by the usual process of driving back and forth through the village! "Why is it, when you ask somebody for directions you always get a local who enjoys putting on such a strong accent, that even his mother wouldn't be able to understand him?" From the car park it is possible to discern a rough track. This leads across two fields, to more open grass slopes, close to the impressive but vegetated and loose Rosen Cliff which extends for 800 metres south-west until it ends at Nare Head.

From here it is possible to descend from the steep grassy apex of the Rosen Cliff down to Lemonia Rock. This cliff eventually becomes a rocky spur, leading straight down to a sloping platform 20 feet or so above the sea. Care should be taken in wet conditions as the friable rock becomes slippery.

THE CLIMBS

The first route is an adventurous outing. It is for those with an aptitude for enjoying loose vegetated rock, that causes consternation and distress.

The Rosen Cliff   300ft *Severe (PP)*   unknown

The slabby area of rock defining the seaward end of the Rosen Cliff has been climbed via a wandering, vegetated line gained from the boulder beach to the south west.

To the east you will find a small zawn. The following routes can be found in the zawn. Two of the routes are on the west face and one on the opposite east face. The routes are accessed by abseil and described starting from the left (west side of zawn) to right (east side of zawn).

Inner Secrets   90ft   *E1 5b (AP)*   1985

Abseil to the foot of the west wall and take a hanging belay. Do this to the left of the small cave which is at the back of the zawn. Climb leftwards to a thin crack leading straight up the wall. It is now possible to finish via a ledge on the left.

Dark Entries   80ft   *E4 6a (AP)*★ 1986

Sport climbers beware! This one is for the traditionalists only. The route is climbed via the overhanging corner in the back of the zawn. Abseil down the corner and make a difficult swing into its base. Climb the wide crack to the roof then move down, out and left around it to gain a niche. On the first ascent a belay was taken at the niche. The rock in particular near the top, should be treated with loving tenderness. Either carry extra large nuts and/or a set of large friends. Or, if neither are readily available, then let your partner lead!

Moving over to the north-east wall of the zawn.

Littlest Racoon   30ft   *Hard Severe 4c (AP)*   1985

Climb the seaward side of the zawn, via the corner.

Continuing north-east, a walk along the coast path from the top of the Rosen Cliff for 200 metres will bring a boulder beach into view. It is bordered on its south-western end by what can only be described as an impressively steep wall. The wall can be seen rising above a diagonal band of overhangs. The following route is found on this wall.

Moonshadow   150ft   *E4 5c (PP)*★★ 1985

A fine climb, perhaps the best on the South Coast. Start below the band of overhangs at the corner.
1: 80ft 5b. Ascend the corner to a point where a loose hand traverse (Peg runner insitu) leads leftwards and enables a curving flake to be reached. Climb this to a ledge and dubious peg belay. Serious.
2: 70ft 5c. Traverse precariously rightwards above the void until awkward moves can be made to a crack line splitting the overhang and wall above. Follow this with difficulty to reach the top.

Immediately opposite the Rosen Cliff, half a mile offshore, is Gull Rock. Romanis also climbed here but noted that it was unpleasant due to the large numbers of sea birds!

First Aid, Helicopter & Rescue notes

THIS IS A climbers' guidebook not a first aid manual! The author and publisher accept no liability for any action that you may take based on these notes. First Aid cannot easily be written down in simple step by step instructions, there are too many variables. Our advice is that you improve your knowledge by attending a course from a recognised source. Courses are run by The St. John Ambulance Service, local authority swimming pools run Lifesaver or Lifeguard courses as do several other organisations. Your local Citizens Advice Bureau can point you in the right direction. *GO AND DO IT NOW,* you might have to save a friend's life one day! The following notes are only intended for your guidance in an emergency if you have no previous knowledge and there is no qualified help immediately at hand.

IF THERE IS AN ACCIDENT AND EMERGENCY

Stay cool, don't panic, block off your own feelings, get on with the job and get the emergency services to the casualty as quickly as possible.

Telephone 999 for the Emergency Services

In the case of a fall or suspected fall do not move the casualty.

Use your mobile phone (some are equipped with an SOS facility) or send someone to telephone for an ambulance immediately, making sure they can inform the operator of the location of the incident and give a correct Ordnance Survey map reference if possible. Also get them to come back and let you know that they have carried out the task.

Saving life is the priority, worrying about spinal injuries will do no good if the victim is not breathing or has no heartbeat. Check quickly (see circulation), but thoroughly, whilst trying to move the victim as little as possible, then act accordingly (see ABC).

REMEMBER — A B C

A – AIRWAY:

If the patient is not breathing:

Check that there is nothing obstructing the airway (i.e., the tongue, false teeth, lumps of blood, sick, helmet strap (loosen the strap, but do not remove the helmet) or anything else that may have found its way in. If after doing all this, the patient does not start breathing: –

B – BREATHING:

Tilt the head back, pinch the nostrils together and place your open mouth over theirs, now breathe out firmly with an adult, but in the case of a small child use approximately half a breath, (do not over inflate) whilst watching to see if the patient's chest rises indicating that the airway is clear. If the chest does not rise, recheck the airway and or, make sure the nose is closed and your mouths are closed together, when you breathe into the patient. Remember to remove your mouth after each breath to allow the patient to expel the air. Use one breath then count five seconds before breathing again, this is sufficient for an adult. Do not stop until they start breathing for themselves.

C – CIRCULATION:

Check for a pulse in the neck. Only if there is no pulse (beware that it is not just a weak pulse).

Lay the patient flat on their back, then place the heel of one hand over the lower end of the breastbone and then place your other hand on top of the first hand, but in the case of a child use only one hand. Now using your body weight, push down sharply and then release the pressure. Use a ratio of 1 breath to 5 compressions, but if you are alone and have to deal with the situation then, use 2 breaths to 15 compressions. Keep checking to see if the patient has a pulse and has started to breathe unaided, if so stop. Keep the patient warm with a blanket or some other form of protection from the cold or wind (even in summer).

HEAD INJURIES:

If you suspect that a climber has received a head injury, then the only course of action is the prevention of further injury and as soon as possible get the patient to hospital.

SPINAL OR NECK INJURY:

This is the tricky one. It can make all other actions in life saving difficult to carry out with speed and confidence. If you suspect a spinal injury in an unconscious victim i.e., having witnessed or suspecting they have just taken a fall, or if you have a conscious victim who complains of pain in the neck or back, shooting pain down the arms, legs, areas of numbness or lack of mobility, then *Do Not Move The Victim Unless To Save Life* e.g., if there is a serious likelihood of further injury to the casualty, yourself, the casualty has no pulse or has stopped breathing and requires you to use resuscitation, REMEMBER TO CALL FOR THE AMBU-LANCE, it is always better to be safe than sorry.

BLEEDING AND FRACTURES:

Do not panic, bleeding can be stopped by direct pressure with the use of a shirt for a dressing, and by elevating the limb.

Suspected fractures, can be dealt with by immobilising the in-jured limb and then getting the patient to hospital as soon as possible.

CLIFF AND SEA ACCIDENTS AND RESCUE

The biggest single enemy in this area of rescue is often fear of embarrassment, the result of years bad reporting in the media! You know the sort of thing, *"They were inexperienced and stupid to go there in the first place said furious coastguards after £60,000 rescue."* In the UK rescue is free provided by you — the taxpayer. Or, in the case of the RNLI lifeboat service by voluntary donation — give generously! Both the coastguard and the RNLI issue 'incident reports' to the media which do not contain judgmental comment. Always veer on the side of caution. The rescue services prefer to be called immediately for a presumed incident and would rather respond to 'a false alarm with good intent' than risk a situation deteriorate. Do not be indecisive.

If you intend to venture onto dangerous or unexplored cliffs make sure family and friends know where you are and when to expect you back. If you are a visitor to the area consider telephoning the coastguard and letting them known your plans, arranging a time to call them back to let them know you are safely off the cliffs. In a rescue situation the best help for the coastguard is knowing where to find you. One major advantage of giving the coastguard an estimated time of return is that the procedure might allow you to stay and nurse an unconscious partner if only two of you have gone out. Remember, the more people who know where you are and what you are doing the safer you will be.

A modern consideration for a rescue aid is a mobile 'phone. Some have a single button emergency facility but in a situation where a casualty is in the water they have one major lifesaving advantage. You can keep sight of the casualty and direct the rescue services from the vantage point of the cliff top. They are still expensive but well worth considering.

IN A COASTAL ACCIDENT AND EMERGENCY

Dial 999 and ask for the coastguard

If there is an accident and assistance is required, dial 999 and ask for the Coastguard. HM Coastguard are the authority responsible for all sea, shore and cliff rescue around Britain. They will co-ordinate the other services such as helicopter, lifeboat and cliff rescue teams once you have alerted them of an emergency.

It is very important to give the exact location of the accident. Give the Ordinance Survey map name and reference of the location and **stress** that this is what you are doing. Local names sometimes differ from map names and are, therefore, more prominent in local minds. Similar names also occur along the coast. Falmouth Coastguard has the choice of two Black Heads for example – in opposite directions. It has been known for rescue teams to go to the wrong location even when correct details have been given for these reasons. If possible have someone to meet the rescue team to guide them to the incident site.

HELICOPTER RESCUE

In the event of a helicopter evacuation **all** climbers **on** or **off** the cliff take heed. A helicopter flying close to the cliff will make verbal communication very difficult and small stones will be dislodged by the rotor down draught. All loose equipment should be secured and climbers in precarious positions should make themselves safe. Never throw a rope to the helicopter. Keep away from the main rotor, the tail rotor and engine exhaust. Assistance should be given to the crew only when requested.

If you are in the water the rescuer will come to you, first coming down in the water away from you. This is because of different static electric potentials, which can be high, before he splashes down. Never make a grab for the crewman's trousers — the results could be shocking! You will be winched up into the helicopter by a thick loop (a strop) placed under your arms. *Keep your arms down by your sides and do not raise them until the winchman has you safely in the helicopter, otherwise you will fall out of the strop.* The crew will get you in and sort you out, leave it to them.

Note: It is hard for a helicopter to spot a casualty in the sea so, if this concerns you, it might be worth investing in a pack of mini-flares. At night a small but powerful waterproof torch or rescue strobe-light is invaluable. However, never use flares when a helicopter is in the vicinity or above the casualty.

COASTEERING & DEEP WATER SOLOING

Traversing above the sea, swimming across zawns or soloing climbs above deep water is tremendous fun. However, far more climbers have died in Cornwall undertaking these activities than while out climbing conventionally. You must have a good understanding of tides and sea states. This is particularly important if a decision is to be made regarding moving a casualty when the only choice may be risking further injury to save them from drowning.

Soloing above the sea provides a false sense of security. An apparently comfortable splash-down can easily turn into a terrifying struggle for survival if you are unable get back onto rock in a heavy sea. Or, if you are taken out by the tide. In a heavy sea it is often better to swim away from the cliffs, you will be easier to rescue farther out as long as you can be seen. If a member of your party is in the water you must *try to keep them in sight,* here is where that mobile 'phone will be invaluable!

You should also be very aware of the *risk of heat loss* if you are undertaking these activities and **never** do so after drinking alcohol.

HYPOTHERMIA

A bad fall into the water can cause both shock and hypothermia. It is most important you understand that even on the hottest summer day too much time in and out of the water will zap your ability to stay warm. It is wise to kit out your sac as you would for the mountains with plenty of spare warm clothes and a thermos of hot soup or drink.

Hypothermia is much more insidious in 'sea-mountaineering' than it is in the hills. Because it can happen to you when it is hot the symptoms are easy to miss and even harder to take seriously. However, you will have been cold and shivery but will have assumed you have warmed up. You may feel warm on the outside but have a kind of dull, numbness on the inside. Your muscles will have a cold dull ache as opposed to feeling 'pumped'. The symptom you are most likely to notice is rapidly increasing lethargy and a realisation that everything is taking you longer to do than it should. You will want to find a sunny slab to go to sleep on. At this point you must force yourself to panic! Dying this way is not unpleasant so you have to get motivated. Tell your friends what you think is happening. Get away from the water. Get on all your spare warm clothes and those warm drinks inside you. Once you are off the crag get as much hot food and drink down as you can and get to bed. If you don't feel you are getting back to normal, get to a doctor.

IMPORTANT: If companions become slow and lethargic while climbing, swimming and traversing etc., they may be exhibiting symptoms of hypothermia. Even if they say they are OK, call it a day and get them warm and fed. Remember, a companion who has had a fall after being cold and wet and is unconscious is also liable to be suffering from hypothermia. Keep the casualty as dry and warm as possible.

Note: additional items of gear coasteers have been known to use include wetsuit jackets and canoeing buoyancy aids complete with whistles, poly survival bags, mini-flares and/or signal strobes. Do not underestimate the value of a whistle. Sound travels well at sea and can be heard long before you can be seen. A whistle blast also has the advantage of being an unusual sound to hear on the sea and has the advantage of prompting curiosity.

Caroline Carpenter bouldering at Downderry.

Photo: Andy Grieve

Sean Hawken coasteering at Pencarrow Head.   *Photo: Andy Grieve*

Hawken's Choice

THESE ROUTES have not been selected by consensus and, therefore, the list is subjective. They are simply routes I have selected, personally finding them to be rewarding and of good quality. This list is intended mainly for the weekend visitor, who may have a limited period of time to spend climbing. With this in mind, my intention is not to spurn all other climbs, but to enable the visitor to taste promptly a selection of worthwhile climbs. I hope, that the majority of climbers will continue to retain a sense of adventure and seek out the many climbs, both with star grades and without, on offer in this guidebook. At certain grades there is a lack of routes, so here I have mentioned the best on offer, rather than no routes at all. The routes are not necessarily in any particular order.

E6

Psychokiller, Cheesewring Quarry. "Hard, hard, like a Mevagissey man."

Strongbow (F7c), Luxulyan Quarry. "Intricate, with a bloody hard crux."

Sweet Surrender (F7c), Cheesewring Quarry. "Thin powerful moves, followed by a superb mantel."

E5

Mauritius, Cheesewring Quarry. "Spectacular, awe-inspiring position!"

Rampage (F7b), Cheesewring Quarry. "One of the best climbs in Cornwall! with a powerful start and an unreal finish."

Special Llama, Kilmar Tor. "Short, overhanging and powerful."

E4

Moonshadow, Nare Head. "The best route on the south-coast."

God Forbid, Roche Rocks. "Gritstone, phoohy. Try this test of true grit!"

Double Agent (F7a), Cheesewring Quarry. "Lovely continuous sequence of moves."

E3

Warrior (F6c), Cheesewring Quarry. "Sport climbing at its best, good moves."

High Noon, Cheesewring Quarry. "A real traditional style challenge."

Treffry Viaduct, Luxulyan. "Eat your heart out Fred Dibner!"

E2

Khyber Wall, Cheesewring Quarry. "Excellent moves, with a real feeling of being out there."

Eyefull Tower, Cheesewring Quarry. "Tough sixties trade route for 'hard men' - Highly technical for the effort-full eighties!"

Purple Haze, Kit Hill. "Excellent crack climbing."

E1

Sleepy Hollow, Kilmar Tor. "Great sequence of knobbly holds."

Mecca, Cheesewring Quarry. "Low pro! Keeps you on your toes right to the end and it keeps getting up-graded too!"

The Lord Falmouth, Roche Rock. "Cool confidence on the technical move to a pleasant, sensational finish."

HARD VERY SEVERE

Simanon Direct, Cheesewring Quarry. "The top pitch is real peachy!"

The Trampoline, Cheesewring Quarry. "High crux and no pro' - stay cool Dude!"

Star Fox, Cheesewring Quarry. "A rather high boulder."

VERY SEVERE

Just Good Friends, Trewartha Tor. "Every move just feels right."

Shorty's Folly, Roche Rock. "A true thoroughbred."

Black Beastie, Hawks Tor. "The beast is out there!"

Porky, Roche Rock. "A direct line and an improvement on a great classic with every move a pleasure."

HARD SEVERE

Purple Revrac, Cheesewring Quarry. "Solid route, with pleasing moves."

Tregagle's Buttress, Roche Rock. "Bold moves for 1921 on the weirdest of rock."

Lemon Tree, Cheesewring Quarry. "Exposed, thought provoking crux."

Figuzzi, Cheesewring Quarry. "The best of several routes put together, great finish."

SEVERE

Ivy-Mantled Tower, Roche Rocks. "Solid rock and an interesting climb."

The Cat's 'ere, Hawk's Tor. "It is! It's out there!"

Mike's Route, Cheesewring Quarry. "A good example of what the grade means in a quarry!"

VERY DIFFICULT

South East Climb, Devil's Jump. "A smashing little adventure."

Scapegoat, Cheesewring Quarry. "The exposure is great, try it with your back to the rock!" (Only joking!)

Peter, Cheesewring Quarry. "First climb in the quarry named by Carver after Stanier, the man who saw the potential. A good introduction to quarry climbing."

DIFFICULT

Fang Q, Hawks Tor. "Beautiful setting and good quality rock."

South East Buttress, Roche Rock. "Great quality rock and enjoyable climbing."

Jane, Cheesewring Quarry. "A good beginner."

HORRIBILIS CAMMIMUS

Now, this list is a little different. Instead of informing you of all the lovely climbs in the area. This list informs you of the routes that ensure your adrenaline runs, as thick brown and sticky stuff. I cannot claim to have tried all of these delectable delights, but when a route becomes a myth you know something's up. Please remember that if you climb much harder than the route is graded, the potential for it to be frightening tends to be far less (sometimes!)

Note: Many of these routes are top quality routes, they're just a little scary that's all!

EXCEPTIONALLY SEVERE (XS)

Dod on Arrival, Dodman Point. "Very Much so!"

E6

Psychokiller, Cheesewring Quarry. "Old bolt-heads and shoe laces for protection."

E5

Bored of the Wrings, Cheesewring Quarry. "Far from boring!"

E4

Dark Entries, Nare Head. "Let your partner go first. Oh, and carry a knife for the belay rope."

Horrorshow, Dodman Point. "Intimidating, by name and nature."

Dead Exit, Cheesewring Quarry. "It's a void, into which only the daring may venture."

E3

High Noon, Cheesewring Quarry. "This could be your High Noon!"

Sex Tips for Monogamous Girls, Dodman Point. "Scary loose rock."

E2

Second Class Return, Cheesewring Quarry. "Grovelling groove, with marginal gear."

E1

Beast of Revelations, Cheesewring Quarry. "Surprisingly popular for a nerve-wracking route."

Divine Comedy, Dodman Point. "Soft rock makes the route very interesting."

HARD VERY SEVERE

Simanon Direct, Cheesewring Quarry. "This route sees more failed attempts than a rabbit with a sperm count of two."

VERY SEVERE

Risky, Cheesewring Quarry. "Unless you have RP's, you're Phucked!"

Direct Route, Cheesewring Quarry. "Screams of despair often resound throughout the quarry, for there are no gear placements."

HARD SEVERE

Traitor's Gate, Cheesewring Quarry. "When seeping, this route is extremely serious."

SEVERE

Fortress Indirect, Cheesewring Quarry. "Very exposed with the chance that one day the whole block may go."

VERY DIFFICULT

Scapegoat, Cheesewring Quarry. "The ledge thins alarmingly at the point of greatest exposure."

LIST OF FIRST ASCENTS
& FIRST RECORDED ASCENTS

1802 August	**The Western Turret**	*T. Bond & Friend*
1802 August	**The Eastern Turret**	*T. Bond & Friend*
1920 July 1	**Chapel Chimney**	*C. B. Jerram*
1920 July 10	**The Circular Climb**	*D. G. Romanis, C. B. Jerram*
1920 July 19	**Black Bottle Rocks**	*D. G. Romanis, C. B. Jerram*
1921	**South East Climb**	*D. G. Romanis, C. B. Jerram*

The classic traditional excursion in South East Cornwall and quite delectable.

North Buttress *D. G. Romanis, C. B. Jerram*

South East Buttress *D. G. Romanis, C. B. Jerram*
A wonderful first route up the buttress. The classic solution.

East Chimney *D. G. Romanis, C. B. Jerram*

Corner & Staircase *D. G. Romanis, C. B. Jerram*

Tregagle's Crack *D. G. Romanis, C. B. Jerram*

Tregagle's Buttress *D. G. Romanis, C. B. Jerram*

Easy Chimney *D. G. Romanis, C. B. Jerram*

1921 Oct. 29	**The Waterfall Slabs**	*D. G. Romanis*

And the first general exploration of Carmears Rocks

1933 August	**Oxford Climb**	*A. D. M. Cox*
1941	**Pinnacle Chimney**	*R. G. Folkard*
	West Chimney	*R. G. Folkard*
	The Roman Nose	*R. G. Folkard*
	Moss Chimney	*R. G. Folkard*
	Diagonal Crack	*R. G. Folkard*
	Rake and Flake	*R. G. Folkard*
	Heather Chimney	*R. G. Folkard*
	Garden Chimney	*R. G. Folkard*
	Crack and Platform	*R. G. Folkard*
	Chimney and Ledge	*R. G. Folkard*
1955	**Ivy-Mantled Tower**	*G. J. Sutton*
1955	**Moping Owl**	*G. J. Sutton*
1955	**Swink Chimney**	*G. J. Sutton*
1955	**Tump Wall**	*G. J. Sutton*
1960s	**Popular climbs, first ascents left unrecorded**	

These climbs, at Cheesewring and on the moor were popular from the mid-1960s onward but first ascents were never claimed. However, D. J. Basset, his friends and members of the Truro School Rock Climbing Club were amongst the first groups to frequent them.

Left Arete

Learner Route

Variation Start

Corner Seat

Central Corner (as an A1 grade Artificial Climb)

The Garden Gate

Garden Wall

Right Arete

Sue

Sarah

Cat Nap

Crack 'n' Up

The Recollection

In August 1964 Cheesewring Quarry was the first significant new crag to be investigated for climbing, in Cornwall, for twenty years. The bold, unprotected nature of the climbing, a marked contrast to natural crags, led to top-rope 'recces' of some 'promising lines' which were named by, and credited to, their 'discoverers.' The ascent date of these few climbs was taken from the date of the top-rope ascent. Where a climb was led by a different climber other than its originator the date has been taken from the first led ascent and the top-rope ascent is also mentioned. The arrival of American pitons early in 1967 afforded greater protection in the quarry so the practice was abandoned. By Easter '67 all the early climbs had been led and a strong preference for 'on-sight' leading had developed.

1964 August	**Peter** *W. A. Carver, P. H. Stanier*
	Direct Route *W. A. Carver*
1965 April 1	**Merlin's Chimney** *W. A. Carver (solo)*
1965 April 1	**Merlin's Traverse** *P. H. Stanier (solo)*
1965 April 5	**The Trampoline** *P. H. Stanier, W. A. Carver*
1965 April 5	**Mecca** *W. A. Carver (crux pitch only.)*

An independent start and finish was added later by Carver with P. H. Stanier (Aug. 27. 1972) to 'tidy up the climb' for the 1973 guide. The present final pitch *The Whit Finish* was added by *W. A. Carver, R. Nadin and P. H. Stanier* on May 27. 1974.

	Anthony *W. A. Carver*
	Traitor's Gate *W. A. Carver*
	Combine *W. A. Carver, P. H. Stanier, Miss A. Lingard*
1965 April 7	**Lemon Tree** *P. H. Stanier, W. A. Carver*
	Simanon Finish *W. A. Carver, P. H. Stanier*
	Thorndyke *W. A. Carver, P. H. Stanier*
1965 Sept. 2	**Fortress Direct** *P. H. Stanier*
	Fortress Indirect *P. H. Stanier*
	Pinnacle Route *P. H. Stanier*
	Scapegoat *P. H. Stanier*
1965 Oct. 17	**Jane** *P. H. Stanier, R. Nadin*

Circa 1960s	**Fang Q** *(First ascent left unrecorded)*
1966 Mar. 26	**Mike's Route** *M. Trethewey*
1966 Mar. 27	**Unnamed** *P. H. Stanier, R. Nadin*
1966 Aug. 14	**Gila's Wall** *W. A. Carver*
1967 Feb. 12	**Juliet's Balcony** *W. A. Carver, S. Bramble*

After which ground-up style becomes absolute for determining first ascent dates and top roped recces are abandoned.

1967 Mar 24	**Eyefull Tower** (2pts of aid) *W. A. Carver, R. J. Grose & P. H. Stanier*

Aid reduced to one point by P. H. Biven on the third ascent, 28 May 1967. Bolt protection added retrospectively 1969. Remaining aid point eliminated by N. Hancock, 8 March 1986.

1967 April 16	**High Noon** (1pt of aid) *W. A. Carver, R. J. Grose*

Bolt protection added retrospectively in 1969. Aid point eliminated by K. Palmer, 8 March 1986.

1967 July 16	**Expensive** (A2) *T. Newberry, T. Benjamin (alt. leads)*

Superceded by a more direct free climb *Special Offer* (1988)

1967 Aug. 6	**Silva Gray** (5pts of aid) *W. A. Carver, R. J. Grose*

Aid reduced to 3 points in May 1975 by W. A. Carver and eliminated completely by A. Grieve and K. Palmer (alt. Leads) July 7 1987.

1967 Sept. 9	**Simanon Direct** *W. A. Carver, R.J. Grose*

Previously top-roped by T. Newberry

1967 Sept. 9	**Northside Route** *W. A. Carver (solo)*

Cornwall's toughest, yet most popular, summit finally gets an ascent without aid or combined tactics.

1968 April 14	**The Vandal** (2pts of aid) *R. J. Grose, P. H Stanier & W. A Carver (Alt.leads)*

Aid points eliminated by A. Grieve, Sept. 16 1986

1968 June 3	**Risky** *T. Newberry, D. Hughes*
	Forty Five *T. Newberry, D. Hughes*
1969 May 31	**Back Breaker** *T. Newberry, K. Appleton*
1969 Aug. 3	**The Purple Revrac** *P. H. Stanier, J. Burley (Alt. leads)*
1969 Aug. 8	**Man of Double Deed** *W. A. Carver, P. H. Stanier*
1969 Aug. 9	**Star Fox** *W. A. Carver, P. H. Stanier*
1969 Sept. 20	**Beast of Revelation** *W. A Carver, J. Burley, B. Hocken*
➡ 1969 Oct. 17	**Bird Line** *M. Bradford, D. Morrod. (A1 top pitch)* ➡

Free climbed by N. Hancock June 8 1985

Circa 1970s	**Figuzzi** Combined quality pitches of other climbs

This pleasing mixture of earlier climbs has proved popular enough to warrant its own description.

1970 Mar 14	**Warrior** (A2) *L. Benstead, S. Chadwick*

First Free Ascent: A. Greive Nov. 4 1988

1970 Mar. 21	**Khyber Wall** (A1) *L. Benstead, D. Morrod*

First Free Ascent: A. Greive Sept. 19 1986

1970 Mar. 21	**Super Indirect** (A2) Pitch 1: *S. Chadwick, B. Wright*
1970 Mar. 27	**Super Indirect** (A2) *S. Chadwick, L. Benstead*

1970 Mar. 30   **Black Panther**   (A3) *L. Benstead, D. Morrod*
1970 April 4   **Corner Route**   *P. H. Stanier, D. J. Cawley*
1970 April 5   **Spectral Radius**   (A2/3) *B. Hocken, I. Rogers*
1970 June 20.   **Gather Darkness**   *W. A. Carver, P. H. Stanier*
1970 April 4   **Corner Climb**   *P. H. Stanier, D. J. Cawley*
1970 Oct 25   **Black Sabbath**   *(A2/3 artificial)*   *S. Chadwick, A. McFarlane (Alternate leads.)*

All aid eliminated on pitch 1 by A. Grieve, June 6 1989 but free climbing the final pitch remains a project.

1971 July 10   **Central Route**   *P. H. Stanier, W. A. Carver.*
1971 May 15   **Shorty's Folly**   *A. Stringer, J. Williams*
1971 Aug. 7   **Central Corner/Pink Panther** (free) *L. Benstead, D. Morrod*

Len Benstead frees a popular 'practise' artificial climb but his new name proves slow to catch on.

1920s/1970s   **The Rosen Cliff**, Nare Head

No first ascent recorded. General explorations D. G. Romanis in the 1920s. W. A. Carver, P. H. Stanier, P. R. Littlejohn, K. Darbyshire in the 1970s.

1972 July 30   **Prince Heathen**   *W. Carver P. Turner*
1972 Sept. 3   **Un-named**   *D. Lord, P. Turner*
1972 Sept 3   **Young Hunting**   (1pt of aid) *W.A. Carver, P.H. Stanier*

Originally climbed by T. Newberry using a top-rope solo technique and 3 points of aid: Aug. 6 1967 but not led. Final aid point eliminated by A. Grieve 1986.

1972 Sept. 16   **Black Jack**   *F. Harvey, J. Williams*
1972 Nov. 11   **Sunset Arete**   *D. Morrod*
1973 April 10   **Horrorshow**   *P. R. Littlejohn, K. Darbyshire*
1973 June 5   **One Way Ticket**   *S. Chadwick*
1974 June 27   **Porky**   *R. Lambourne, M. Dunning*
1974 Aug. 11   **Sentry Box**   *R. Lambourne, M. Dunning*
1974 Dec. 28   **East Face**   *R. Lambourne T. Mason*

A 'forced' rest was taken on a nut during the first ascent. A. Grieve and C. Rees climbed the line on June 8 1985 mistaking it for a new climb and naming it *Bullfighter*. Their ascent dispensed with the rest, increasing the grade.

Circa 1975   **Cue**   *R. Hart (solo)*
                Cue 2 *R. Hart (solo)*
                Barney   *R. Hart (solo)*
                McGrew *R. Hart (solo)*
                Cuthbert *R. Hart (solo)*
                Dribble   *R. Hart (solo)*
                Grub *R. Hart (solo)*
                Florence *R. Hart (solo)*
                Zebedee *R. Hart (solo)*
                Dougal   *R. Hart (solo)*

Dylan *R. Hart (solo)*
Divers' Route *R. Hart (solo)*

1975 Feb. 23   **Summer Soldier** (A1) *M. Dunning, T. Mason*
A historically significant Cheesewring climb. Toni Carver, committed to the belief that the climb would go free, made many attempts on the line. Martin Dunning prepared simply to climb it also made several attempts before sorting out suitable gear for his aid ascent. Shortly afterwards all new routing activity ceased here for almost a decade. When it resumed this climb became Andy Grieve's focus for pushing up the grades and it fell to him as a free climb which he renamed *Trouble with Lichen*.

1975 Sept. 1   **South Face Route** *T. Mason R. Lambourne*
1975   **Rene** (A1) *D. Morrod*
First Free Ascent: L. Earnshaw, circa 1991.

1976 Sept. 4   **Second Class Return** *T. Mason, R. Lambourne*
1984 Sept. 18   **Kit Hill Killer** *P. O'Sullivan, K. Tole*
1985 April 19   **Trouble with Lichen** *A. Grieve*
1985 June 8   **Beau Peep** *K. Palmer, N. Hancock*
1985 Oct. 10   **Inner Secrets** *A. Grieve N. Hancock*
1985 Oct. 23   **Moonshadow** *A. Grieve N. Hancock*
1985 Nov. 23   **Littlest Racoon** *W. Goodyer, P. Saunders*
1986 Mar. 8   **Dark Entries** *A. Grieve N. Hancock*
1986 April 6   **Purple Haze** *A. Grieve*
1986 May 9   **Nocturne** *A. Grieve*
1986 May 27   **A Whole Lotta Shakin' Goin' On** *K. Palmer*
1986 Summer   **Dead Exit** *N. Hancock*
The summer of '86 saw a determined campaign to eliminate all aid moves on the old traditional climbs at Cheesewring by Hancock, Palmer and Grieve leaving *Eyefull Tower, High Noon, The Vandal, Young Hunting* and *Khyber Wall* entirely free climbs.

1986 May 28   **Half Man Half Biscuit** *A. Watt, N. Hancock, K. Palmer*
1986   **Sarah Louise** *C. Rees*
1986 Aug. 30   **Chocolate Orange** *A. Grieve*
1986 Sept. 23   **TDK** *A. Grieve, K. Palmer*
1986 Sept. 26   **Mirror Mirror** *A. Grieve, C. Rees*
1986 Sept. 9   **Agent Provocateur** *K. Palmer, N. Hancock, A. Grieve.*
1986 Oct. 4   **Hamamelis** *A. Grieve*
1986 Oct. 4   **Barbecue Wood** *A. Grieve, C. Rees*
1986 Oct. 11   **Garfield's Gut** *N. Hancock*
1986 Oct. 11   **Jood The Zood** *N. Hancock, P. Saunders*
1986 Oct. 11   **Splitting Images** *A. Grieve, N. Hancock, P. Saunders*
1987   **Half Route Half Boulder Problem** *N. Hancock (solo)*
1987 May 5   **True Grit** *A. Grieve*
1987   **Simian** *A. Grieve*

1988 May 14	**Special Offer** *A. Grieve*	
1988	**Psychokiller** *S. Mayers*	
1988	**Wring the Changes** *S. Mayers*	
1988	**Children in Need** *Ascensionists not currently known.*	
1988 Nov. 4	**Chance** *C. Rees (Solo)*	
1988 Nov. 4	**Bump Start** unrecorded	
1989 May 5	**Bored of the Rings** *A. Grieve*	
1989	**Mauritius** *K. Palmer*	
1989	**Wall Flower** *L. Earnshaw (First recorded ascent)*	
1989	**Cheese Disease** *L. Earnshaw*	
1989	**Moss Trap** *P. Matthews*	
1989	**Drippy & Strangely Brown** *L. Earnshaw, D. Gillard*	
1989	**Titch** *D. Gillard, L. Earnshaw*	
1989	**Blackberry Wall** *P. Matthews*	
1989 Dec. 9	**Snap Happy** *A. Grieve, C. Rees*	
1989	**Sex Tips For Monogamous Girls** *C. Rees, A. Grieve*	
1990	**Chocolate Hobnob** *L. Earnshaw*	
1990 June 6	**Dwarf's Dream** *S. Hawken (solo)*	
1990	**Sheep Shit Shooter** *L. Earnshaw*	
1990	**Special Llama** *K. Palmer, C. Rees*	
1991	**Dod on Arrival** *C. Rees (un-seconded)*	

1991   **Dod on Arrival** *C. Rees (un-seconded)*
The only climb to merit the Exceptionally Severe (XS) grade in this guidebook.

1991 April	**On Mirkwood Edge** *D. Turnbull, A.Grieve.*	
Circa 1991	**Left Feeling a Little Queer** *L. Earnshaw*	
	Infelation *L. Earnshaw*	
	Long Rock Climb *L.Earnshaw (Solo)*	
	Shlong *L. Earnshaw*	
	The Queen of Rock *L. Earnshaw*	
1991	**In God We Trust** *L. Earnshaw A.Grieve*	
1991	**PMC** *Plymouth College boys*	
1991	**The Fang Direct** *C.Rees*	
1991	**Fang Arete** *C. Rees*	
1991	**Treffry Viaduct** *C. Rees, A. Grieve*	
1991	**Captain Webb** *C. Rees*	

1991   **Captain Webb** *C. Rees*
"One crazy dude!"

1992 Oct. 13   **Fingerbob** *S. Hawken*
M. Roscorle belayed but did not follow.

1993	**Double Agent** *A. Grieve*	
1993	**Debutante** *S. Golly*	

1993 June   **Real Live Wire** *A. Grieve*
S. Golly belayed but did not follow

1993 June   **Gone to Pot** A. Grieve

A passing American gentleman, Mr. B. Zook, belayed but declined to follow.

1993 June 5	**Rabbit Arete** *S. Hawken, C. Carpenter*
1993 July 5	**Potential Energy** *S. Hawken* K Martin belayed but did not follow.
1993 Sept. 3	**Volker's Visit** *V. Kelme*
1993 Sept. 3	**Khyber Pass** *S. Hawken* Caroline Carpenter held Mr. Hawken's.....ropes, but declined to follow.
1993 Sept.	**Rampage** *A. Grieve, S. Golly*
1993 Sept.	**Fox Glove Arete** *A. Martin, S. Lornie*
1994 Jan. 1	**Friend or Foe?** *A. Grieve* S. Hawken held the ropes.
1994 June 6	**Nomadic Jam Session** *S. Hawken* C. Carpenter belayed.
1994 July 24	**Tag** *S. Hawken* L. Earnshaw belayed.
1994 July 24	**Watchman** *S. Hawken* C. Carpenter belayed
1994 July 24	**Feline Adventures** *L. Earnshaw, S. Hawken*
1994 Sept. 5	**Snatch** *S. Hawken, C. Carpenter*
1994 Sept. 8	**Sidekick** *S. Hawken, C. Carpenter*
1994 Sept. 14	**God Forbid** *A. Grieve, S. Hawken*
1994 Oct. 13	**Cosmic Joker** *S. Hawken* C. Carpenter belayed
1995 April 8	**Crucifier** *S. Hawken* C. Carpenter belayed
1995 April	**Bouncy Bouncy Kangaroo** *A. Grieve, N. Hancock*
1995 May 1	**Sleepy Hollow** *S. Hawken, M. Rescorle*
1995 May 13	**Game On** *L. Earnshaw, R. Clayton*
1995 May 13	**Hullabuloo** *L. Earnshaw, R. Clayton*
1995 May 13	**Aretion** *L. Earnshaw, R. Clayton* Bob Lambourne recalls making an ascent of an arete in the Luxulyan Valley in the late '70s/early '80s with Rob Walker. He never found out if the climb was on Carmears Rocks or not! The feature that sticks in his mind is having first to climb an '8ft piece of steel embedded almost vertically in the ground' to gain the arete. The memory implies that the pair may have made the first ascent of the Aretion/Hullabaloo pinnacle.
1995 June 12	**Sweet Surrender** *S. Hawken* (M. Rescorle belayed)
1995 June	**Sling Shot** *A. Grieve, N. Hancock*
1995 July 3	**Black Beastie** *S. Hawken, A. Grieve*
1995 July 3	**Just Good Friends** *M. Rescorle, A. Grieve*
1995 July 4	**Bloody Helman** *S. Hawken, A. Grieve*
1995 July 6	**Le Tour** *A. Grieve, S. Hawken*

1995 July 13	**Hot Lava** *A. Grieve* S. Hawken belayed
1995 July 18	**The Cat's 'ere** *M. Rescorle (solo)* First Recorded Ascent
1995 July 21	**Big Black Pussy** *T. Catterall, S. Hawken*
1995 July 21	**Pumping Panthers** *S. Hawken, T. Catterall*
1995 July 21	**Jugular Vein** *T. Catterall, S. Hawken*
1995 July 21	**Highly Clawsable** *S. Hawken, T. Catterall*
1995 July 21	**The Darkness Beckons** *A. Grieve, S. Hawken*
1995 July 21	**La De Dah** *M. Rescorle (solo)*
1995 Summer	**My Life Led Up To This** *N. Hancock, A. Grieve*
1995 August	**Daisy's Flapjack** *A. Grieve, M. Rescorle*
1995 August	**The Crystal Maze** *A. Grieve* (M. Rescorle belayed)
1995 August	**Total Recall** *S. Lornie (First Recorded Ascent)*
1995 August	**West Point** *M. Rescorle, S. Hawken*
1995 Oct. 19	**Hell's Tooth** *I. Parnell, S. Hawken*
1996 Jan. 2	**Divine Comedy** *S. Hawken, A. Grieve*
1996 Feb. 2	**The Go Between** *N. Hancock, L. Earnshaw*
1996 Feb. 2	**Overhanging Crack** *L. Earnshaw, S. Blagdon,* *N. Hancock*
1996 Feb. 2	**The Long Drop** *N. Hancock*
1996 May	**Longshang's Leap** *T. Carver (solo)*
1996 May	**Heart of Darkness** *T. Carver, W. A. Carver (alt. leads)*
1996 May	**Steps Arete** *W. A. Carver (First Recorded Ascent-solo)* An old novices' top rope pitch which, surprisingly, no one had bothered to record a lead of!
1996 May 28	**Double Trouble** *A. Grieve, S. Hawken*
1996 Aug. 22	**In Cod We Trust** *T. Catterall (solo)*
1996 Aug. 22	**Captain Birdseye** *T. Catterall (solo)*
1996 Sept. 28	**Rubble Without a Cause** *S. Hawken*
1996 Sept. 28	**Grim Reefer** *T. Catterall* S. Hawken belayed but did not follow
1996 Aug. 8	**Strongbow** *A. Grieve* S. Hawken belayed but did not follow
1996 Sept. 9	**Chicken in the Rough** *S. Hawken, A. Grieve*
1996 Sept. 24	**Pooh Pooh** *S. Hawken, A. Grieve*
1996 Oct 23	**'Our Carver'** *S. Hawken, A. Grieve (alt. leads)*
1997 May	**The Lord Falmouth** *W. A. Carver* (solo) Toni Carver did not think this a new climb but that it was well worth including when he made this first recorded ascent in the process of checking route descriptions for this guidebook.

INDEX OF CLIMBS